7.50

The
Sermon on
the Mount

Dr. J van Bruggen

The Sermon on the Mount

a travel guide for christians

PREMIER PUBLISHING
WINNIPEG, 1986

Bruggen, J. van, 1936—
    The Sermon on the mount

    Translation of: De Bergrede.
    ISBN 0-88756-033-4

1. Sermon on the mount — Criticism, interpretation, etc.
I. Title
BT380.2.B7813 1986   226'.906   C86-098089-8

First Printing – December, 1986
Second Printing – November, 1989
Third Printing – January, 1993

PREMIER PRINTING
ONE BEGHIN AVE., WINNIPEG, MANITOBA, CANADA R2J 3X5

Foreword

The Sermon on the Mount represents one of the most well-known sections of the Bible. Many people think that the speech forms Christianity's constitution for all ages. This great respect for Jesus' basic teaching tends to go hand-in-hand with a certain feeling of embarassment. Christians seem to be at a loss as to how to bring the Sermon on the Mount into everyday life: can you convert its gold into currency for underway?

This book delves into that question. It offers an exegetical discussion of Jesus' speech. The text of Matthew 5 to 7 is discussed section by section with an emphasis on searching for the core of Jesus' teaching crucial for the Christian life. The Sermon on the Mount marks the route to God's kingdom. While reading it we not only need to look at the text in front of us but we also need to pay attention to the path upon which we as listeners are placed. I hope that the discussion of the Sermon on the Mount offered here can help young and old when using Jesus' compass on the journey of faith.

Appended to this book is a study guide for further Bible reading centered around the Sermon on the Mount.

Kampen, the Netherlands, 1986 Jakob van Bruggen

Table of Contents

1. Faith is Obedience

> Seeing the crowds . . . . He opened His mouth and taught them.
>
> Matthew 5:1-2

Faith as experience?

There was a time when faith was a given. Everyone knew that a person ought to believe. For the most part it was clear what a person was supposed to believe and how he was supposed to live. Unbelief became associated with underdeveloped peoples. An un-Christian life was a barbarian one.

That time is now past. Faith is still tolerated, but why should faith be considered any better than unbelief? Living a Christian life is permissible but only as a private matter: public life has become neutral, dechristianized.

Many people today experience faith as a neutral matter too. Within Christianity emphasis is shifting more and more towards the *experience* of faith. If the experience of faith is real and personal, a person can believe anything he wants. Attention in the Christian life moves from the fixed norms to personal choice and personal responsibility. The question of how something is viewed or experienced becomes more important than the question of what it is or ought to be.

As a matter of course the Christian faith also loses its exclusive character. Why shouldn't Muslims, Jews and Buddhists have genuine faith-experiences too? Missionary work aiming at conversion has been traded in for dialogue which leads to understanding.

For many in the 20th Century a shared faith means: sharing experiences of faith. Faith is free, isn't it? In this way faith becomes neutral. The only surviving heresy is the demand that others believe a particular doctrine and comply to a certain lifestyle. Doesn't the very nature of faith exclude every kind of authority, whether it be the authority of a church, a confession or a Bible? One clear issue appears to have survived in our obscure and vague era: faith is free.

Faith as obedience

The New Testament speaks of faith in a different way. In his first epistle the Apostle Peter talks about obeying the truth (1:22), and he is not the only one. Paul, in his letter to the Romans, says that the apostles have been sent out to call all the nations to obedience to the faith (15:18, 1:5, 16:26). The word obedience indicates that faith is not a neutral matter: believing means submitting.

We cannot say that a later development shows up here in which the frozen doctrine of the apostles smothers Jesus' spontaneous gospel of love. Jesus Himself taught them that believing is the same thing as obeying, even unto death. When Jesus sent the 12 disciples out for the first time during His earthly ministry, He gave them a set of instructions for believers: "He that loveth father or mother more than me is not worthy of me: and he that loveth son or daughter more than me is not worthy of me. And he that taketh not his cross, and followeth after me, is not worthy of me. He that findeth his life shall lose it: and he that loseth his life for my sake shall find it." (Matthew 10:37-39) Believing has more to do with the behavior of a loyal soldier who is ready to die for his king than with the reports and experiences of an observer at the front. The apostles are in perfect harmony with their Master when they call faith obedience.

Jesus' own appearance on earth let this be felt too. Right from the very beginning.

All kinds of people

After Herod Antipas imprisoned John the Baptist, his preaching was continued by Jesus. It started in Galilee, in the North of Palestine. He addressed Himself to the whole people of Israel. His message was meant for everyone, and this included the miraculous healings. Matthew writes that "Jesus went about all Galilee, teaching in their synagogues, and preaching the gospel of the kingdom, and healing all manner of sickness and all manner of disease among the people," (4:23). Inevitably, people poured in from every direction to experience Jesus' work, sometimes in their own bodies. Soon masses of people from the whole of Palestine were following after Him. Matthew watches as they stream forth from Galilee, the Decapolis, Jerusalem, Judea and from beyond the Jordan (4:25). Jesus isn't for a hand full of people or for certain character-types. He seeks the nation, humanity. Faith is something for everyone.

Once the crowds have come together Jesus appears to expect something from them. They have been attracted by the experience of His miracles. Now He pulls them along in His wake. Seeing the crowds arriving, He went ahead of them to the mountain. Matthew assumes that his readers already know that Jesus had a particular mountain retreat (5:1). This mountain, situated northeast of the Sea of Galilee, served as His base. To Him and His disciples this was *the* mountain: Jesus' well-known mountain. The mountain is not new. New, however, is that Jesus' base now becomes the meeting place for the people of Israel. With Jesus they cannot remain neutral. He precedes them as guide and is leading them somewhere.

The journey is striking. Matthew says that He went up on a mountainside(5:1). Translators often write that Jesus climbed up the mountain, but that is not the case at all. Matthew indicates that Jesus went up to the mountain in the same way that pilgrims went up to Jerusalem each year. Traveling together to the city is self-evident. The temple is located there, isn't it? But why would anyone take crowds from the whole of Israel up to a mountain: does Jesus have more to offer there than at the earthly Jerusalem? At the beginning of His ministry Jesus is already focusing all sorts of people's attention on a destination towards which they all have to follow Him obediently. Whoever comes to Jesus, notices that He takes control of the direction of life!

Wanted: disciples

Having arrived at the mountain the crowds are not allowed to remain neutral. They have begun to follow and now they must become disciples. Jesus sits down in the manner of a teacher in Israel and Matthew tells that His disciples come to Him (5:1). Solemnly and officially the teaching begins. Matthew chooses almost ceremonious words to indicate that: "And He opened His mouth and taught them, saying" (5:2).

This instruction is meant for all kinds of people. The multitude has not been brought along in vain. Jesus provides His teaching for them (Matthew 7:29). It isn't instruction for a select few. At the same time the lesson-plan very plainly indicates that no neutral, open-air gathering is being held either. The disciples are standing or sitting in front of Him for a purpose:

Jesus wants to be surrounded by followers and every listener must learn how to be or become a good disciple.

Luke's Gospel contains a fairly short summary of the Sermon on the Mount (6:20-49). Most striking is Luke's focus on the parts of Jesus' teaching which directly concern the requirements for a disciple. Luke has apparently trimmed down the Sermon on the Mount in order to clearly show Theophilus and other readers that it is the rule of learning to live the Christian life. Matthew provides a more complete text. He too records all sorts of passages in which Jesus directly speaks to the Jews of His day. Still, Matthew's rendering demonstrates that the whole sermon's theme is how to be a disciple of Jesus. It is a lesson in learning how to follow. Faith is not neutral. Believers can only remain erect by hearing Jesus' words and by doing them (Matthew 7:24). All sorts of different people have to learn one single kind of obedience. For that reason Jesus took them up to the mountain.

The Sermon on the Mount's significance can certainly be seen in the preparations of the night before. Luke (6:12-19) tells that Jesus remained awake between the arrival at the mountain and the preaching of the sermon. It is the only time that we read about a whole night filled with prayer. Jesus began to preach His commands only after having spent hours on His knees pleading with the Father for the people. Early the next morning He designated twelve as disciples who would always remain with Him. In this way the circle of followers became a kind of nation with a council of twelve. The blueprints for a new people, gathered around Jesus, begin to take shape, and after that Jesus descends to a level place by the mountain in order to heal the sick and to deliver His speech to the disciples and listeners. Even the preparations show that Jesus intends to take all these people into service for a great future. The faith-experience surrounding the healings is supposed to be translated into faith-obedience to Jesus' commands.

God's authority

Familiarity with the Sermon on the Mount often obscures its most wondrous element. There is no question that the first listeners heard it correctly: Jesus teaches with authority and not like the scribes. They were amazed at this (Matthew 7:29). They even remained talking about it later: "What thing is this — what new doctrine is this?" (Mark 1:27). The harmony of Jesus' teaching was obviously in another key. The scribes appealed to the laws of Moses and the prophets to support their assertions. Only the Lord God has authority. Men can only repeat things. For that reason the scribes give their instruction in a tone of submission. Doubly striking is that Jesus does not appear as an expositor of the Bible in the Sermon on the Mount: there are hardly any references to the Old Testament. Jesus talks as if He Himself is the giver of law. Quite characteristic is His statement: "But I tell you." In the Sermon on the Mount Jesus Himself is speaking: "Verily I say unto you." He commands and the people are bound to His commandments. Apparently the Creator, the LORD Himself, is standing in front of the disciples, not a man from Nazareth.

This tone belongs to the revelation in the Sermon on the Mount. Jesus lets the crowds from Israel know who He is. His miracles already pointed in a definite direction. Now He is also speaking without reservation in the manner of God the Law-Giver. Faith-experience must become obedience because Jesus is nobody less than God's own Son, who became man. The mystery behind this authority is the mystery behind Jesus' person.

The Sermon on the Mount is full of commandments because the person delivering it is the one Master to whom every mortal being is subjected, even in Israel. Faith has become a neutral affair for many in the 20th Century. This, in turn, stems from the 19th Century's rejection of belief in Jesus' conception by the Holy Spirit as well as any belief in Jesus' divinity. Why should the teaching of a fellow human being from Palestine have any more authority than other doctrines present in the world? The opposite, however, applies as well: whoever recognizes Jesus as the Christ, the Son of the living God, understands that faith in this Jesus cannot be neutral. It demands submission. The tone of the Sermon on the Mount reveals the voice of the Good Shepherd. The Shepherd has authority because He is the master and gives His life for the sheep. Now we have to follow, regardless how narrow the way He leads may be.

The enduring Sermon on the Mount

The mountain towards which Jesus led the crowds is now deserted. The speech delivered there at the beginning of Jesus' earthly ministry remains among us. Matthew and Luke have preserved its major elements in their Gospels, and not as a report of something that happened once in the past but as the rendering of what Jesus asks of all kinds of people during all ages. The sermon has permanent validity.

Its validity has been watered down in many ways. The commandments of the Sermon on the Mount are only supposed to apply in a millennial kingdom yet to come. Or, they are not applicable to all people, but only to those who cherish lofty ideals. Or, they are really only intended to let us see how imperfect we all are. In this way the Sermon on the Mount becomes a museum piece for the church rather than a marching order for today.

There are certainly enough indications to maintain that Jesus' teaching is also applicable for later periods. The whole sermon is set in an unconditional tone and formulated as broadly as possible. Later in the Gospels we find parts of the instruction just as they are given in the Sermon on the Mount: it is constantly repeated and impressed upon the reader. After His resurrection Jesus called the disciples to the mountain where He had given His commandments and He commissioned them to make disciples of all nations and to teach them to obey everything which He had said (Matthew 28:16-20). Apparently the question what Jesus had actually commanded His disciples was closed at the end of Matthew's Gospel. He had written it down earlier in the book and, in particular, in the Sermon on the Mount. As well, we should not be surprised to discover that James' Epistle is soaked into the Sermon on the Mount and that the author sometimes quotes it word for word in order to keep the church on the right path.

The Sermon on the Mount has always remained popular, at least some parts of it. Certain sections are eagerly employed to support disarmament and oppose nuclear weapons, to support aid for the Third World and to oppose the capitalist system. We shall yet see to what extent the Sermon on the Mount really does provide pointers in this direction. However, beginning a political or social debate on the basis of one or two texts from the Sermon on the Mount is senseless without first recognizing that the whole Sermon has authority over us and demands our obedience. We cannot reject the faith and then turn around and use texts from the Sermon on the Mount as slogans at a demonstration.

Listening to this teaching is something quite different than plucking out quotes.

The Sermon on the Mount has not been given in order to spruce up our ideals. Having received it, we must subject our whole life to it. Jesus compares the man who hears and obeys these words with someone who builds his house on a rock. The choice of the building site was not free: it had to be this foundation. A person may intend to erect a home for his fellow man even though he builds outside it. But the flood rains will wash it away because the house is built upon sand.

Anyone beginning with life, building a house, has to start with listening and obeying. It's possible: God's only Son has come in order to show us the way. Believing is obeying, but obeying is also believing: believing in the Good Shepherd.

2. Happiness

Blessed the poor in spirit:
theirs is the kingdom of heaven!

Matthew 5:3-12

Ideals

Every human heart knows the longing for a happiness yet unattained. For that reason men, in contrast to animals, look expectantly to the future. Ideals, once conceived, bring about dissatisfaction, revolt and bitterness when they are not realized. Since many things turn out differently than we expected and since death is moving towards us, a layer of hardness, aggression, egotism and jealously spreads over many human hearts. Deeply hidden the longing for a better happiness, another life, remains. Having originally come from Paradise people can never be totally happy in the present-day world, and on account of that they often make each other very unhappy.

Surprisingly, Jesus now begins His instruction to the people with a discussion about happiness. He knows that people, even when they are not unhappy, do not yet possess a happiness without blemishes. Before unmasking our shortcomings in oftentimes strong language, He speaks to our heart which restlessly longs for perfect happiness. A whole series of Beatitudes surrounds us with road signs pointing to real peace. Jesus wants to make men into His disciples because He wants to give them the unattainable. He is the Savior. His commandments bring happiness.

Happiness is divine

Despite having rebelled against God and then having been expelled from Paradise, man nevertheless has a notion about a happy life, even though he doesn't have any idea of what it might be. Too often happiness is seen as a point at which all of our desires, wants and needs are satisfied (as if anybody lived on Easy Street!).

In the Beatitudes Jesus reminds us that we lost peace and happiness in Paradise. We can only recover them by relocating the trail to God. Every Beatitude consists of two lines. The second line describes what kind of happiness we can expect with Jesus. Blessed, happy, are the poor in spirit, for theirs is the kingdom of heaven.

The kingdom of heaven is not the same thing as heaven. The kingdom of heaven is a term describing the place where heaven calls the tune. It is sometimes called the Kingdom of God: the area where He has the upper hand. The world of humanity has truly become a human's world, more and more turned away from God. But it won't remain that way. God will come again to subdue this rebellious province and place it under the authority of heaven. That had already been promised to our forefathers when they were expelled from Paradise, and this promise was often repeated in the Old Testament in all kinds of ways. Finally, John the Baptist arrived as the herald of the approaching kingdom of heaven. Now that Jesus appears the future is near. His death for the sins of men will lift the blockade. The time is now dawning in which men may once again inherit God's Paradise through faith. A new order will soon unfold: the never ending era of a humanity coming to full development through heavenly living on earth. Happy is the man who experiences that.

This desire for happiness does not cut us off from the earth. On the contrary, it reunites us on this planet with God: the only One really capable of making a man happy forever because He Himself is life, light and joy.

The concluding phrase of the first Beatitude determines the pitch of the one which immediately follows. A certain rounding-off is achieved in verse 10 while the same concluding phrase returns once again: "Blessed are those who are persecuted because of righteousness, for theirs is the kingdom of heaven." People will never become happy by trying to leave heaven outside of things. Jesus brings us happiness by reconciling us to God in heaven.

Looking at the Beatitudes between verse 3 and verse 10, we discover that every second line gives a certain description of this kingdom of heaven. There people will be comforted: God is drying the tears which now sometimes flow without end.

Then we will inherit the earth: mother earth, torn open by changing world powers, can breathe again. When the meek rule, the lion and the lamb can lie down together.

Then we will be satisfied with righteousness: every human

existence falls short now, but then it will breathe only innocence.

We will be shown mercy: those who demanded their rights and sacrificed others to get them, will now come into a world in which everyone will pull themselves up by grace.

There we will see God: it isn't possible now. Even the sun is far too strong for our gaze, and we sometimes look down in the presence of a really good man. Imagine how much we will be changed when we see God Himself: pure life and light!

We shall also be called children of God: a new existence will start. No more human life in and of itself. God's name will be inscribed on their deeds. Our name will change from child of man to child of God.

That is the kingdom of heaven: that's happiness, and Jesus stands for that. The curse which lies over this life will be lifted. The veil of death will be taken away. Happy the disciples of Jesus: for theirs is the kingdom of heaven.

Happiness must grow

People who demand their rights want happiness delivered today, immediately and already put together. They forget that happiness lives, and everything that lives grows. To be happy with the fruits, you first have to be happy with the seeds. They forget something else as well: sometimes happiness has to be restored because it was broken. That recovery needs time and sacrifice. A broken marriage can be made happy again, but the person who damaged it may not demand that happiness. He may work for it, hope for it. Having gone through difficult times it can still return like a gift, different and deeper. But this happiness does not grow without contrition and repentance.

Now this also applies to the real happiness which God gives. Having accumulated a record of guilt, we are, even in the best of circumstances only a tiny bit aware of the injustice and sorrow we have inflicted on our good Creator. Our understanding of that still has to ripen. But we are given the time for that. God does not move us from a corroded life into a perfect existence by the wave of a magic wand. He takes His time and follows a certain path. The restoration of happiness here demands growth in repentance and trust. Not as a precondition for receiving happiness but as the essential precondition for *being* happy. How can a life without contrition and belief ever be suitable ground for a divinely, happy life? Many prison inmates first have to pass through a program of rehabilitation before taking their place in the society (which stands ready to receive them). When God's grace opens the gates to the kingdom of heaven for us, we must first undergo reeducation to make us mature enough for this happy world. In this regard the crucial factor is not the length, but rather the depth. To be really happy we have to be willing to change.

For that reason each Beatitude consists of two lines: the second line points to the happiness, while the first line notes for whom this happiness is reserved. It is for the poor of spirit, the meek, the merciful and the persecuted. All of these descriptions point in the direction which we should now live. The road to heavenly happiness travels along the following stations: humbly hoping in God and unpretentiously loving our neighbor. Jesus does not describe these conditions for happiness as a kind of hurdle which we first have to clear. He does not say that we will be happy after having first passed a test of poverty and mercy. He simply says that we are already happy while underway as poor of spirit and persecuted. Happy because we are already standing on the road to a heavenly life. We are already growing in the right direction. Recovery has begun and God will insure a complete cure.

The most well-known exhortation is to be poor in spirit. This call applies to both rich and poor. Jesus uses a word that does not indicate the poor, but rather the destitute beggar. Beggars like this still exist, and in some lands there are scores of them. They beg for food. But very few people are spiritual beggars: when the angels look out of the windows in heaven, do they see many human hands and human souls held up begging to God? How many men have a deep sense of their total poverty and guilt before God and plead for His grace? Still, it has to begin here. Jesus pointed Israel in this direction. He came as a healer and they streamed to Him with pitiful cries for help: Have mercy on our crippled, blind and demon-possessed! and Jesus helps. But then leading the same people to His mountain He sits down in order to teach them that happiness will come when they turn to Him like beggars for their spirits and souls and not just for their physical ailments. Happiness from God, which can only be obtained by begging, is only for those who no longer seek happiness in themselves.

Following the first Beatitude about the poor in spirit come

three others which touch upon our relationship to God and another three which are concerned with our neighbor. In verse 4 Jesus calls those who mourn blessed. He uses a verb which is related to mourners. Jesus does not mean that it is pleasant to lose a loved one through death. He teaches us, in prosperity and adversity, a bearing which is necessary for real happiness. Not the attitude of the complacent who are very satisfied with themselves, but the bearing of those who are in mourning for their sins. John the Baptist already stated it clearly enough: we must repent of our sins when the Lord approaches. Jesus can now be short. Blessed are those who took John's appeal to heart. Blessed are those who are disappointed with themselves, who kneel before God in sackcloth and ashes: They have already started out on the road back to happiness.

In verse 5 Jesus calls the meek blessed. In this regard He does not have certain character types in mind, but those who do not seek to obtain their rights with insolence and violence. Having become humble, they let God lead their lives. The meek appear to get the worst of it in this life where only the fittest survive. But Jesus encourages them. The strongest will not end up on top, neither the most insolent, nor the most wicked: the future of the world is not booty which we can conquer but an inheritance which has to be willed to us. God designates the meek as the legal heirs of life. After all, they have expected it from Him and not from themselves.

In verse 6 Jesus terms as blessed those who hunger and thirst after righteousness. A lot of people might appear to be able to stand in line for this one. Doesn't every political party work towards righteousness on earth? But then we need to be careful not to overlook Jesus' choice of words. He uses an unfamiliar phrase: hunger and thirst. That refers to food and drink, things our own bodies need. Strangely enough, people outside of Paradise are always talking about righteousness, while hardly ever recognizing that their own lives are devoid of it. John the Baptist pointed that out, even to the religious pharisees. He taught the people that their own stomachs needed to be filled through a baptism of repentance: their lives lacked any righteousness. Many of John the Baptist's disciples are now sitting around Jesus, and He calls them blessed when they have discovered their unrighteousness and when they long for forgiveness and sanctification. They are standing on the road to happiness. For happiness can only come back into the world via the hearts of the children of men: Not through revolution, nor through war, but through conversion to God.

The reality of this subjection and humble relationship of faith to God must be evident in a loving attitude towards our neighbors. In verse 7 to 9 Jesus gives the following characterizations: merciful (not returning evil for evil), pure of heart (dealing with one's neighbor on the basis of selfless motives), peacemaking (not asserting one's rights or causing strife). We have to bring these three words into our lives. Then it will become clear that we are really humble before God: why stumble over our neighbor's petty faults when so much more has been forgiven us? We are beginning to grow towards happiness: the heartbeat of all happiness is the love which is from and through God.

Happiness carries

Jesus' words about persecution receive an extra, personal accent. He speaks more broadly about this when verse 10 is worked out in verses 11 and 12. Apparently nothing is finer than to be persecuted and hated for Jesus' sake. "Rejoice and be glad, because great is your reward in heaven. For in the same way they persecuted the prophets who were before you." Why should this be an encouragement? Isn't it demoralizing that that opposition and insult will never end? On the contrary, these things will come to an end. The prophets said that one day the Savior would come, and they were persecuted on account of the hate for the coming Messiah. Now the promised Messiah does come: the hate bursting forth proves that with Jesus we are at the right address. His name may be slandered, but through it we know that the promised one is finally standing before us. Satan, who appeared to have won in Paradise, attacks Him violently. But now that He has come the issue is close to being settled. Winter is over: rejoice, summer is returning!

Jesus commands happiness, even in persecution. That seems strange. How can you order someone to be happy? His command truly shows that the final triumph is certain. The general who instructs his troops to raise the song of victory knows what he is doing. Fighting remains to be done, but the victory banners are already being unfurled. The command demands trust. In Jesus and His Word. Just as the Beatitudes call for faith. Jesus does not change our lives behind our backs. He speaks to us with promises. Isn't that an intentional delay? No, for how could people be happy without first having lost the contorted bearing of unbelief?

3. Israel

> You are the salt of the earth. If salt has lost its taste, how shall its saltness be restored? It is no longer good for anything except to be thrown out and trodden under foot by men.
>
> Matthew 5:13-16

The people

For many people, certainly in this day and age, faith is closely bound up with special attention for Israel, the Jewish people. Aren't the Jews the Christians' "older brothers" and isn't the Old Testament in the first instance the book of the people of Israel? The establishment and development of the modern Israeli state following 1948 gave strong, new impulses to these feelings. Despite this state's un-Christian character and to a certain extent hostility to Christianity, many people still watch it with eager expectation: will God make Israel the focal point of the nations in a kind of a thousand-year kingdom? Many feel that God cannot get along without Israel, certainly not for good.

God's history has certainly granted this people a special position. But not from the start. God has been writing world history from the very first day. His concern focuses on the nations, not only before but also after the flood. He ranks no nation above the other. But when the nations continue their steadfast rejection of God after the construction of the tower of Babel and the confusion of the languages, the Lord searches for a small base from which He can operate in the rest of the world. Abram is called. God's purpose remains opening a way to the nations and does not mark the beginning of a nationalistic tendency in His work. Abram, the father of Israel, will be called Abraham, the father of many nations. Through him all the nations of the earth will be blessed. This was Israel's beginning: the nations remained the goal while this one nation became an instrument to reach them. Henceforth God lands His gifts on this base. The Law of God, good for all people, is entrusted to Moses. The promise of a King who will bless the earth, reaches the house of David. In this way Israel became the nation that had something unique to offer: wisdom of God. Even the Queen of Sheba comes to obtain it. In the first century AD the Jews were quite conscious of their position. Paul describes it as follows "You are convinced that you are a guide for the blind, a light for those who are in the dark, an instructor of the foolish, a teacher of infants, because you have in the law the embodiment of knowledge and truth" (Romans 2:17-21).

Jesus confirms this special position in the Sermon on the Mount. He turns to the crowds from Israel and says without any reservations: "You are the salt of the earth; you are the light of the world." These words are not limited to the disciples of Jesus. Threat and exhortation accompany them as well. The whole of the Sermon on the Mount is instruction of the crowds and Jesus would certainly have spoken more conditionally (as He did in verse 11) if He had only intended to address His remarks to the people who had become His disciples. Having arrived on earth Jesus begins with Israel too. God has built a city on a hill there: Jerusalem, Zion, the beacon for the world, and there in His law, God has kindled the light which now shines on the lampstand, on the menorah Israel, for the nations everywhere where synagogues are located. God's Son begins with the one nation to which God pulled back in history in order that He might win back all the nations through it.

The light of the world

In His words directed to Israel Jesus shows how God intends to reach the nations. The title "Salt of the earth" is not a compliment. No one eats salt in and of itself. Salt is esteemed when it makes other food tasty. Light does not exist as an entity all by itself: it is not thriftily saved by being hid under the corn bushel found somewhere in every Middle Eastern house. Light is valued because we can see each other with it: in the one room apartment common in the Orient everyone sees everyone else present thanks to the light. Salt and light exist for their surroundings. Thus an out-of-order Israel immediately becomes uninteresting and useless to the world.

Jesus' statements represent a continuation of all kinds of things said by the prophets of the Old Testament. Their uniqueness here comes from their connection to the Beatitudes which just preceded them. Forming a kind of postscript for the Beatitudes, verses 13 to 16 become even sharper for the people.

Verses 3 to 12 clarify how the salt of the earth should taste: it should taste like Jesus. It is also clear what color the light should be: it has to spread the glory of Christ. The call to be meek and even to be persecuted for Jesus' sake lands right in the middle of a people that up to now had the function of a lighthouse in the world. This nation's task now becomes making known and confessing to the world the Son of God, sent to Israel. The healings and miracles so brilliantly performed among the people, particularly among this people, are intended to activate them to be world-salt and world-light.

The good works Israel is supposed to demonstrate to the world are the good works of the Beatitudes, the works of faith in the Messiah who has come and is sovereign: He is the light of the world, and He has come to Israel. May this people grasp its calling for humanity anew.

This call is not neutral. Jesus links a veiled threat to it: tasteless salt will be thrown out the door as worthless, just like so much garbage in the Orient which lands on the street only to be trampled underfoot. Jesus employs a striking expression. He speaks about salt that "has become foolish." In this way we know that He is talking about people, not salt. A people can become "foolish" by rejecting Jesus. If that people just happens to be the salt of the earth, they become tasteless too. They will be trampled underfoot. This happened: in the year 70AD the city on the hill fell to the besieging Romans. Consequently, the Jewish people, in so far as they remained un-Christian, have no longer any significance in leading the nations to God's kingdom. The people as nation, instead of God's kingdom, came to stand in the lime-light. But what is salt without taste? What purpose does a lampstand, a menorah, have, when the Light of the world, Jesus Christ, has no place on it? Jesus issues a timely warning to preserve Israel from national meaninglessness. For that reason He exhorts the people in the Sermon on the Mount: accept and mirror God's light in the darkness!

The nations

Jesus' words contain not only a veiled threat, but also an open encouragement. A city which God builds and a fire which He kindles cannot remain hidden. He makes sure of that Himself. When the nations default following the flood, He lights a flame in Israel and constructs Zion. When Israel turns its back on Jesus,

God insures that some Jews still believe and He adds to them many Christians from other nations. The Christian church remains secured.

This church, the renewed Israel gathered by faith, also falls under the law of salt and light. In the new covenant the church has sometimes acted as if it had intrinsic importance. When that occurs Jesus' word becomes arousing and threatening power against the church too: tasteless salt is thrown away and light must shine if it is to have any significance. The issue was neither the glory of the people of Israel then, nor is it the honor of new Israel now. Only one thing is important: that other people see God's light through us and glorify our heavenly Father.

That happened too: by holding high the light of Christ's gospel Peter and the other apostles brought many pagans to kneel before God the Father and His Son Jesus Christ.

It has to continue in this way. The gospel is not an alibi, but a task. In and of itself the church is of no importance. The only thing that counts in this world is the glory of God.

4. The Bible as Building-Program

> I have come not to abolish the law or the prophets
> but to fulfill them.
>
> Matthew 5:17-20

Faith and the Bible

Over the past few centuries stock in the Bible has fallen sharply in price. Nevertheless, many people want to continue to believe in one way or another. After all, you have to keep the faith. This faith then attaches itself to a few, self-selected texts or sections from the Bible. Of course, the only authoritative passages are those which mean something to me. Can you force someone else to believe because another person says it is so or simply because it's there in the Bible? On this basis Biblical scholarship has come to stand critically over and against the Bible as a whole (the Canon) and over and against subsections of it in particular: Only those portions which can stand the scrutiny of our Biblical criticism are allowed to command any respect. From this same position dogmatic theology has distanced itself strongly from the historical confessions of the church: truth can only be truth when it's true to me, right? In the final analysis these developments declare the authority of the Bible as God's Word to be undone. "Faith" liberates itself from the Bible as God's book.

Living in the 20th Century, we ought to be struck by the fact that Jesus Himself upheld the whole Bible. He says: "Do not think that I have come to abolish the Law or the Prophets." His listeners might draw this quick conclusion because they did not understand why Jesus taught them with such divine authority. Does He intend to replace the law and the prophets with something else? Israel lived according to the Law of Moses and the Prophets of the Old Covenant. That was their Bible, which was referred to as "the law" or the "law and the prophets." Jesus' authority neither pushes out nor replaces that Bible. On the contrary! Although the Pharisees quickly insinuate that Jesus comes in the name of the devil, He himself never tires of showing the people how the Scriptures witness of Him: He holds fast to the Bible.

When Jesus searches out and accepts in love people who are living contrary to the Bible, like prostitutes, tax collectors and sinners, He leaves absolutely no room for misunderstanding: He orders them to cease their sinning. He does not cut any corners with the Bible of God. Faith in Jesus does not push the Bible into second place.

Jesus Himself puts the Bible into first place. He says: "I have come to fulfill the law." It is not the case that Jesus avoids any conflict with the law and prophets. Instead He is what they intended, He fills them up. Faith in Jesus then means that we also have to take the whole Bible seriously.

The Bible and history

But can you take a 2000-year-old book seriously as if it were current and modern in the 20th Century? Hasn't the progress of history turned the Bible into an outdated book from the world of yesterday? We might think in this way by forgetting that the Bible is genuinely a prophetic book. Since prophets inspired by heaven, are speaking, their words reach further than their own time. Yes, the Bible certainly comes from the day before yesterday, but it extends beyond the day after tomorrow.

Jesus presupposes this when He comes to fulfill the law and the prophets. In the book from ancient times the news is recorded which still has to take place and Jesus is coming to make it a reality. "Not the smallest letter, not the least stroke of a pen will by any means disappear from the law until everything is accomplished." The letters will be transformed into events right down to the smallest details.

We could compare it to a building-program for history in which God builds an ideal world and does not abandon His plan even after our rebellion. It does, however, form a long route of stagnation and opposition. In this way the report about God's building plan and of its advancement also becomes longer and longer too. We pass Cain and the generation of the flood, the builders of the tower of Babel, the great apostasy in Israel and the sinful kings. When John the Baptist finally appears as the herald of the Messiah, we have not come any further than the call to conversion: repent! The history of the construction comprises above all a story about unending strikes and industrial sabotage. Nevertheless, God's plan continues to direct the progress. Then Jesus comes with a promise guaranteeing its completion: "I tell you the truth, until heaven and earth disappear, not the smallest letter, not the least stroke of a pen will by any means disappear from the law." The kingdom of heaven will one day come into view, and we can be very sure of it thanks to Jesus' oath. He takes it upon Himself to complete God's plan to bring this world back to the original Paradise. Not even a cosmic weapon of destruction can prevent that.

Many people view the Bible too statically. As if it was a still life. But the picture stirs and is moving towards a future. Much has already been fulfilled and translated into real life. The sacrificial laws have been fulfilled in Jesus who offered Himself as a complete atonement for our sins once and for all. Prophecy was fulfilled when He was like a lamb that is silent before its shearers. Many things from the law and prophets are no longer just the letter: they have become flesh in Jesus Christ. Other things still have to be fulfilled. The mountains have not yet brought any peace and the little hills righteousness, as the Psalmist promises. We may look forward to that. The Bible is a travel guide and we are already over the halfway mark. Thanks to Jesus a book from yesterday brings us to the time of tomorrow.

Bible and conversion

Jesus' work to make the Bible reality also has consequences for the reality of our own lives. He makes certain that the kingdom of heaven is coming. There people shall again become great. There they will rule with Christ and they will pass judgment, even over the angels. Only through Jesus are little, measly men able to make such a glorious appearance later. In order to become great in the kingdom of heaven, we must also be willing to become small with this Jesus who was crucified.

Only those who teach and do "these smallest commandments" will be called great in God's kingdom. The text does not say, as some translations suggest, "one of the least of these commandments." It says: "One of these smallest commandments." Jesus refers back to His own commandments just as He had given them in the Beatitudes: poor, humble, merciful, and willing to be persecuted. These are only small things compared to the assignments which are waiting for us in the kingdom of God. One only stands to lose by it. Faith is the single thing which we can win through it, and that treasure is the point of it all. We can enter God's kingdom alone through faith and that faith becomes apparent when we take upon ourselves the small and inglorious commandments given by Jesus in the Beatitudes. Whoever considers that beneath him has no worth in the kingdom of heaven. But those who do that, will be called great.

The scribes and the pharisees instructed the people in the commandments of the law and the prophets. That was the right thing for them . But now Israel has to move on. They also have to add the commandments of Jesus to what they learned in the rabbinic school. Whoever goes no further than the rabbis, misses the Messiah and His law. Whoever believes in Jesus and takes up His smallest commandments, reaches the destination set out by the law and the prophets.

Faith is more than receiving and passing on Jesus' teaching; more than accepting the New Testament alongside the Old. Faith means that we "teach and do" these things. Jesus puts doing in the first place. We are inserted into His building program. There's no other way.

Building programs and specifications are really only interesting at building sites. In this way the Bible is not a pulp novel for commuters, but a guide to conversion for sinners. Jesus upholds this by binding the law, the prophets and His own commandments to our hearts. Anyone who keeps the Bible, whether whole or in part, outside his life and belief, will inevitably lose the channel on which God broadcasts.

5. Dealing with Others

> I say to you that every one who is angry with his
> brother shall be liable to the council
>
> Matthew 5:21-26

Social consciousness

In our day and age the creation of a social conscience oc-
cupies a large place in secondary education and in all kinds of
courses and training sessions. This stress focuses upon personal
consciousness-raising. Man should learn to see himself primarily in terms of his relationship to others. Strangely enough, this
emphasis on relationships can produce the unexpected side-effect
that our neighbor quickly disappears from view. In reality the
issue no longer concerns my neighbor, but *my* relationship to
him or her. Whenever the quality of this relationship is lacking,
or when no relationship is able to be built up at all, all sorts of
people are abandoned in the name of the quality of life. Unborn
children are aborted while elderly who appear to have no relationship with their surroundings are turned over to "euthanasia."
These borderline cases in our society, at birth and in old age,
testify to the fact that the relationship with our neighbor is in
a deep crisis. The increasing conflicts between various groups
and races shows this as well. When relationships are disrupted,
for example, between a government and its citizens or among
the inhabitants of a certain locality, then the choice for "civil
disobedience" or support for the Ku Klux Klan quickly becomes
a reality.

Endangered species

Our social conscience does not sufficiently protect our fellow-
man. God then did not turn our neighbor over to us. He has
placed this neighbor under the protection of His Law. The Ten
Commandments say: "Thou shalt not kill." Certain kinds of
animals have been declared to be endangered species, but no
one less than God declares man himself to be an "endangered
species." God stands in front of our neighbor, looks us straight
in the eye and orders us to keep our hands to ourselves. The

Sixth Commandment does not forbid the administration of justice or the death penalty: the verb employed in the Hebrew deals with murder and manslaughter. Primitive revenge and passion are forbidden here. The tendency of man to behave like that is less apparent as long as there is rule of law. But the moment rule of law disappears "civilized" man can suddenly become cruel to his neighbor. In milieus where respect of the rule of law is weak, the stiletto often makes a quick appearance.

The Sixth Commandment doesn't pay us any compliments. Perfect people do not have to be forbidden to kill each other. Apparently we need a commandment like this. Cain already proves it. In his case we can see that man's evil nature is deadliest to those closest to him. The commandment is given within the fellowship of the people of Israel. And Jesus warns about being angry with your own brother. Those who are near to us sometimes hear the harshest things. God wishes to protect this neighbor as brother, friend or co-worker: God Himself defends those we most easily turn against.

Beloved weaker brothers

Jesus sharply focuses this protection of our neighbor in the Sermon on the Mount. Everyone knew from the Old Testament that a murderer was subject to judgment. Jesus now goes further in his instruction. He says that even those who are mad at their brother must stand trial. Jesus shows that this is not a figure of speech by providing two examples which follow: whoever calls his brother "Raca" (empty head) is answerable to the Sanhedrin. This must have seemed like an outlandish assertion to the Jews. The Sanhedrin, the highest court in Israel, could leave murder cases to lower, regional courts. How absurd for someone to land in front of the highest court in Jerusalem for a minor offense (an insult)! and just as strange is the second example. Whoever says "you fool" will be in danger of the fires of hell. Murderers in Israel earned an earthly death through stoning. Does a minor offence (a slur) really result in a much severer sentence, namely eternal death? Using this shocking statement Jesus lets His listeners know how seriously God views unloving behavior towards their neighbor. Most people don't think it is very bad to hurt someone just a little bit. After all, it's not a fatal blow. Jesus teaches just the opposite. The issue is not whether we spare our neighbor the worst, but whether we wish him the best! The commandment forbidding killing is intended in a positive sense: You are required to do only good things for your neighbor. God Himself demands this kind of a positive attitude.

Interestingly enough, the two examples given in the general rule of verse 22a concern people who are mentally or physically weaker than we are. Fools and idiots. It's easy to put down those who are in some way inferior to us. Thereby we can see how arrogance and pride are firmly rooted in our hearts. This pride permeates the nations which call others "underdeveloped" and people who consider everyone else to have an "inferior education," or from a "lower social class" or have a "limited intelligence." This putting-down of our neighbor, often-times unnoticed, is a deep source of suffering, friction and strife. Jesus teaches us another attitude. Insults hurt! He teaches us love and respect for our neighbor, even when they might be mentally deficient or less-endowed. Real love does not look down on someone, but stands next to him. Jesus Himself went to live among sinners in this way. He did not revile, and He who was strong, became weak for our sake. We may not approach our neighbor with anything less than this kind of love.

Reconciliation

Jesus knows that we sin against this love. Sometimes we remember that our neighbor justifiably has something against us (verse 23). God's commandment then demands both a sense of guilt and reconciliation. People constantly accusing one another are often satisfied with the expression: "Let bygones be bygones." But when dealing with God, real reconciliation is demanded. Not only is a protected neighbor hurt, but our conduct saddens the protecting God as well.

Reconciliation has two parts. First, with our neighbor to whom we confess that we have said or done something wrong. A prayer of forgiveness directed to God without this confession is null and void. Jesus underlines this sharply: better to let the priest in the temple wait at the altar, then to let your brother wait for your confession of sin. Nevertheless, reconciliation to our neighbor is not enough. Some modern theologians allow reconciliation with God to disappear into a reconciliation with our fellow man. Jesus, however, says that we still have to bring our sacrifice to God after reconciling to our neighbor. Our humility before our neighbor is completed with a humble prayer of confession before God. In this way we learn to deal with one another before the watching eye of God.

It is important to keep this in mind. Coping with one another still takes place in public: a neighbor whom we hold in contempt is in fact busy writing out our summons for the last judgment. As long as we are on earth, walking on the same path, let us reconcile to one another on time and let us be friendly to one another instead of hurling insults. Otherwise our fellowman will become our accuser, and the judge to whom he delivers us is the legislator of the Sixth Commandment. At the last judgment He will enforce the commandment to love one another. The question whether we shall vindicate ourselves to our fellow-man will only be definitively answered by God at the judgment. For that reason reconciliation is a matter of life and death.

Preparing for the kingdom of heaven

By sharpening the 6th Commandment in verses 22 to 26 Jesus shows that He upholds the commandment given to Moses, but that at the same time He brings a more penetrating teaching to the people who are listening at the mountain. His authority continues to speak, connecting up to the Law of Sinai.

This earnest exhortation has everything to do with the coming kingdom of heaven. The era of perfect love is standing at the door. Those who actually believe that, need to start practicing right away. Those who fail to put off insults and learn friendliness for Jesus' sake, will fall further and further behind. Whoever believes that heaven is at hand, will learn to conduct himself differently with his neighbor. Jesus is concerned with that faith. It helps our neighbor and saves our own life.

6. Marriage and Faithfulness

> I say to you that every one who looks at a woman lustfully has already committed adultery with her in his heart.
>
> Matthew 5:27-31

Matrimony is original

Marriage as a life-long commitment of a man and a woman appears to have become outmoded to the Western mind. In practice many still choose it but they are forbidden to view this as exclusive or even the most preferable kind of life-style. The only thing original and creative is the love relationship. Marriage is supposed to be an artificial, super-imposed form. This vision gnaws away at marriages within our society by undermining their very foundation: the characteristics of marriage, physical union and living together, are easily cut loose from one another. Life-long faithfulness which is essential for married couples goes up in smoke in countless divorces. Statistically the preference for marriage may be increasing again, but in many cases such marriages are simply a shell of what they are supposed to be. Nevertheless, there is nothing in this world so original and genuine as marriage. The history of mankind began with the wedding of Adam and Eve. The law of marriage was formulated at that time: "For this reason a man will leave his father and mother and be united to his wife, and they will become one flesh." The word "united" points to a permanent commitment: man and woman become one flesh within a life-long covenant. Neither before nor outside of it. God has placed man far above the animals in this. Animals experience casual relationships and only in special cases does a relationship last a long time. Men, on the other hand, are allowed to surround their desires and feelings with will and understanding. This forms a protection. The pitcher of love can be filled until it bursts, but marital faithfulness keeps even a broken pitcher watertight.

Marriage as a communion of love and faithfulness, self-denial and patience, is very original: it reflects some of the love which is in God. In Christ he continuously loves a church of sinners.

This love endures, suffers, and bears, always and forever. We are allowed to catch a glimpse of these reflections in human marriage whenever it really is a marriage: a life-long commitment to fidelity in love.

In Paradise the Seventh Commandment remained superfluous. Marriage certainly existed but unfaithfulness never even reached the horizons of the heart. After we had fallen away from God it was necessary to call man to order, now unfaithful to his fellow-man as well: "Thou shalt not commit adultery." In the Sermon on the Mount Jesus repeats this prohibition and He points to three things threatening marriage: infidelity, dishonesty and negligence.

Infidelity

Infidelity to one's spouse is commonplace in this world. The novel development in our time is the attempt to expunge the appropriate word out of man's consciousness. All kinds of neutral-sounding expressions have come to take its place: open-marriage, wife-swapping, plurality of life-styles and so on. But there is only one appropriate word when a man is not faithful to his wife or a wife to her husband: infidelity! Moving or liberating experiences are irrelevant: the real question is what has been shattered or broken in the meantime. A husband or wife has been sacrificed to adultery. This breaks the marriage's back, and God forbids it without exception. He chooses sides for the other party: you may not break open either your own marriage or the marriage of another!

The Old Testament contains instructions for a ceremony to be held in the Temple when a husband suspects his wife of adultery (Numbers 5). At issue here is the suspicion and not the reality of infidelity. Nevertheless, the ceremony which follows is gripping. It looks like a funeral service: the wife appears with hair undone, the husband comes with a food offering of barley flour, a drink containing dust from the temple is mixed, and a throw-away clay jar is employed instead of a copper pitcher. The temple mourns when even the suspicion of adultery casts a shadow over a marriage, and that temple shows us God's countenance. Great sorrow follows the loss of beautiful things!

Dishonesty

In the Sermon on the Mount Jesus upholds the Seventh Commandment: Thou shalt not commit adultery. He goes even further by forbidding adultery in our thoughts and even the suggestion of it in our behavior. "Anyone who looks at a woman lustfully has already committed adultery with her in his heart." Here He is thinking of eye contact. A man trying to catch the attention of another man's woman. Life is full of dubious glances, gestures with double meanings, and sexually loaded words or contacts. The feminist complaint about the way in which women are molested in the work-place is not without foundation. At the same time these complaints are not taken very seriously because most people see a big difference between rape reported in the newspapers and passes made at the water fountain. Humanly speaking there is a great deal of difference between the two. Interestingly enough, Jesus places them both on one line. Both are condemned as adultery.

The essence of adultery, of course, is a lack of faithfulness. This comes from the heart. For that reason it is just as bad when this kind of infidelity remains inside the heart and a person succeeds in controlling his unfaithfulness by confining himself to dishonest gazes or contacts. The marriage remains intact, but pureness and uprightness are missing, and that has consequences. A marriage is written with the heart: the script fades when the heart is dishonest. The real question is not what can be experienced in terms of adventure and pleasure, but what is broken down in terms of honesty and quality in the relationship of husband and wife.

Negligence

Negligence represents a third threat to marriage. Jesus points to this by discussing the Jewish practice of sending a wife away with a letter of divorce in certain situations. Proponents appealed to the Law of Moses for support. Deuteronomy 24 does speak about a letter of divorce. Nevertheless, the Jews employed this chapter very selfishly. Moses really says no more than that a man may not take his first wife back after he has sent her away and remarried. In the meantime she has become the wife of another. Moses did not institute the letter of divorce, but he tolerated it and also gave rules limiting its use. The language of these limited rules seemed to escape the Jews: They began to treat the letter of divorce as a normal transaction. Jesus shocked them by bringing an end to the right of the letter of divorce as well. What Moses tolerated, Jesus abolishes. Its time is over.

Why does Jesus as Law-giver go further than Moses? Because He wants love and fidelity to increase on the eve of the kingdom of heaven, and anyone who gives his wife a letter of divorce without adultery as the cause insures that she will commit adultery. Jesus' argumentation is quite striking. Until that time no one gave much thought to what happened to the other party after the divorce. Just as long as your *own* reputation remained unsoiled! But Jesus knows that a divorced wife, and certainly in a time without social welfare, is almost forced to marry another. Is that her fault? Or did her husband's actions give her no other choice?

Jesus' words presuppose a marriage's insolubility. No one is allowed to shirk his responsibility to the other. Not only is marriage threatened by infidelity, but by negligence as well. This needs to be stressed in a time when couples "go their separate ways" without the marriage having been pulled apart by adultery. No one appears to get hurt and each person is only responsible for the way in which he or she goes on to fill in life after the separation. This chain of thought exists only by the grace of marital negligence. Whoever lets go of someone else, is not home free if the other person later stumbles. Weren't they both called to help, support and protect one another until death separated them?

Over and against negligence stands responsibility. Loving in faithfulness knows no end to responsibility. Taking up the task of protecting a husband or wife, regardless of the cost, is preparation for the kingdom of heaven. This kingdom is ours because Christ was responsible for us unto death.

Marriage and the kingdom of heaven

Although appearing to be quite severe, Jesus' commandments for marriage are in reality filled with hope. If the world only knew infidelity and meanness, there would be little point in pursuing love and faithfulness. But if a world characterized by love and faithfulness exists, then it is worth the effort to aim at that world. Jesus can press for strong marriages because the reality which they foreshadow is fast approaching. The kingdom of heaven is the never-ending marriage feast of the Lamb!

For this reason Jesus also gives serious commandments to

all those who believe in that kingdom. Not because every marriage is equally easy for those who believe, but because God's judgment touches our marriage and everything which preceded it. The crossroads leading to heaven or hell are certainly bound up with the acceptance of God's commandments concerning marital fidelity. In verses 29 and 30 Jesus mentions the possibility that our whole body may be thrown into hell. The physical lives of men receive a lot of attention these days. But this is short-sighted attention. Anyone who truly loves his body does well to submit it to God's commandments. Only in this way will our physical existence be saved from the fire and be spared for full blossoming in God's kingdom.

Self-discipline

In the Sermon on the Mount Jesus calls self-discipline a weapon in the struggle against infidelity, dishonesty and negligence. He assumes that His disciples have not yet reached perfection. Their eye or their hand could lead them into sin today. Weak is our will and fickle our desire. But now the question remains whether we have resigned ourselves to that or whether we try to struggle with ourselves for Jesus' sake. This demands self-discipline: "If your right eye causes you to sin, gouge it out and throw it away. It is better for you to loose one part of your body than for your whole body to be thrown into hell." Jesus' statement could not have been meant literally. How does plucking out an eye help us? The other one could just as easily lead us into sin, couldn't it? The point here is to keep every part of our bodies under control. That we turn our eyes away when it's necessary, and that we restrain our hands in order to remain honest and pure in our actions. The expressions which Jesus employs remind us of cruel punishments sometimes imposed upon criminals (gouging out an eye, cutting off a hand). Who would ever do such a thing to himself? Keeping yourself in check and denying yourself things on account of fidelity to someone else seems totally absurd in an age in which man is taught to experience everything. Jesus, in fact, teaches us that we can only hold on to the other person when we are willing to let go of ourselves. That we can only live with God when we rid ourselves of many things we love. Not because we are ascetics or because we flee from the world, but because taking part in a great expedition means leaving a lot of baggage at home.

We can see many beautiful things with our eyes and there is much we would like to reach out and hold, but entrance into God's new world demands self-denial and self-control. A Christian appreciation of film, literature or dance today increasingly involves a conscious distancing from all kinds of movies, books and styles of dance because they directly or indirectly aim at sexual infidelity. Abstention may be unpopular. But the person who does not know when to cut into his own flesh, will not blossom soon either. The marriage feast after the last judgment is worth more than a few parties before death. Better to stand aside for awhile today, than to be cut out of things for good tomorrow.

7. Honesty

> Let what you say be simply 'Yes' or 'No'; anything
> more than this comes from the evil one.
>
> Matthew 5:33-37

On my oath!

Telling the truth does not speak for itself among men.
Whenever testimony has to be given, a judge wrings it out with
an oath. Apparently man has to be placed outside of his normal
way of speaking in order to ascertain the truth. Compelled by
God he does so, but not on his own.

Even when God's name remains unmentioned, an oath in
our society always reminds people of the existence of Someone
above man to whom everyone is responsible. No one can mislead
Him, and He hates the lie. Penalties for perjury betrays that man
still has a notion of a world in which only the truth belongs.

In this way, too, it was impressed on the people of Israel that
an oath must be kept. If promised under oath, it had to be fulfilled
before God's eyes. Thus Israel learned that only truth can stand
in front of God. Before Him the truth speaks for itself.

Yes, no, maybe

No one speaks under oath in ordinary conversation. Neither
does this part of life appear to need an oath. It has its own rules
of conduct and codes of communication. The stringent rules applied to an oath or perjury do not matter here. In fact, dishonest
expressions or untrustworthy actions spring up all over: from
the "white lie" to falsely filling in a form, and some forms of
dishonesty are generally accepted. A weakened conscience can
even make the black market white.

The Jews in Jesus' day had developed certain pseudo-oaths
which were of lesser weight than the oath before God. They
swore by heaven, by the earth, Jerusalem or by the hair on their
head. While making some assertions more believable, oaths like
that also lessened the risk of a subsequent accusation of perjury
when things somehow went wrong. The result was differentia-
tion in the quality of truth.

In this way words lose more and more of their power in our contact with one another. We say "yes" or "no" to our neighbor, but what is it worth? The quality of our speaking determines the value of our contact with one another. In the Sermon on the Mount Jesus commands us to always let "yes" be "yes." The commandment presupposes a great deficit in this regard.

Sometimes people replace "yes" or "no" with "maybe." That is a vague word which keeps a person non-committal: "Maybe I'll come by" (but do we ever intend to do it or do we already know that we are not going to come?). Young people use evasive answers to camouflage their actions from their parents, and by providing vague information a husband isolates himself from his wife. An air of reduced trust comes to hang in families and marriages as a result. The lack of clarity, an unreserved "yes" or "no" in daily contact, can finally result in the silence of negation, in concealment and suppression.

Sometimes, however, we hear solid, clear words. "Yes" and "no" are spoken aloud but later they appear not to have been meant. Just said in passing. Then a girl feels her trust in young men ebbing away because she discovered early on that "yes" does not necessarily mean "yes" at all, and once disillusioned, is twice apathetic or shy. A "yes" not a "yes" or a "no" not a "no" opens a larger wound than a dagger or a revolver: the soul rather than the body has been injured.

The father of lies

Jesus teaches that all of this comes from the evil one. Satan began his work amidst us with an insinuation in Paradise: he awakened the evil thought that God might be less good for man than it appeared, and the lie still characterizes Satan's work. He also scatters the seeds of mistrust which quickly take root among people, and this seed is hidden in the words. Jesus attributes every form of dishonesty to Satan.

Many evasive words or dishonest acts have been placed in a kind of no-man's land: Things taking place in the gray zone between oath and lie. Maybe it's not right, but why should it be wrong? With His word Jesus sweeps this middle ground right off the map. It doesn't exist. The world is situated in the line of fire between God and Satan, truth and lie. Whoever believes that there is a neutral zone outside of strict honesty is mistaken.

Whatever cannot bear the light of the oath, lies in the shadow of our enemy.

Drastic pronouncements like these shake us awake. Only a sincere "yes" or "no" is appropriate in God's kingdom. Nothing is ambiguous in the kingdom of heaven. Everything is crystal-clear there. Surprising and unexpected perhaps, but never disappointing. We are allowed to orient ourselves to that kingdom: we have to be its citizens.

This means that we have to be upright in our contact with family and friends, and that we must be faithful to promises and honor them. Finally, that we are serious in our association with others. Upright, faithful and serious: anything else comes from the evil one!

Talking in God's world

The oath brings us before God's invisible throne. Our daily life may appear to be far removed from it. That, however, is an error. Jesus teaches us otherwise: we always stand right in front of God whenever we speak. We cannot keep Him at a distance by running away from an oath. He is there and close by.

Jesus reminds us that the world is His creation in which He lives. Heaven is the throne of God and earth the footstool for His feet. By looking up, we are staring at His palace. Although we cannot look inside, His eyes look down at us from it. Not in order to spy like satellites do. But to love and to save. The sun, moon and stars take turns as lamps always burning on the forecourt of the palace. God's leading and power have complete control over everything which happens on that forecourt: the earth can only revolt underneath His feet! We need to realize where we are located whenever we speak with one another. With God we cannot just run outside and look for our own spot.

God not only rules here but He is also active in saving sinners. Jerusalem is built here, the city of the great king. In Jesus' day there was no king in Jerusalem, but the great king was expected there. God sent that great king too: Jesus. God's truth does not float above the earth but has become flesh in our midst. Whoever talks with his neighbor, speaks in the same world in which God's Son died and was resurrected. We cannot equivocate with the truth in surroundings where He suffered for that truth. Peter wept bitter tears when he realized that he had lied in the very place where the Master was being struck for his sins.

God's reality touches every man personally. Some young people have difficulty bridging the gap between church and their own room. The latter appears to be in a different world: your own room where you like to be yourself in between your own books and your own music. God's truth appears to be light years away from the surroundings in which we are primarily searching for our own identity and where we want to experience everything authentically. But Jesus then reminds us that we are still incapable of making one hair on our heads white or black. Some people appear to be able to color their hair a solid black, or red or purple. But that is an illusion, and that is man's strong point: giving another appearance to things and above all to himself. With what right do we do that now? Let everyone look in the mirror and ask who has in reality determined the color of his hair. Our identity is ultimately God's creation. He made the specific person that I am, with my facial expressions, posture and hair color. God is this intimate with each person. Our hands, formed by God right up to our very personal finger-tips, should begin to shake violently whenever our tongue derails and speaks dishonestly. Through God we live, move and exist. Every impure tone immediately sounds false in God's personal presence. Since we live from God's breath, we ought to do nothing other than deal honestly with one another. We live under oath!

8. Disarmament

> I say to you: Do not resist the evil one. But if any
> one strikes you on the right cheek, turn to him the
> other also.
>
> Matthew 5:38-42

The peace movement

In the Sermon on the Mount we hear Jesus speaking about non-violence: "If someone strikes you on the right cheek, turn to him the other also. And if someone forces you to go one mile, go with him two miles." Aggression calls forth aggression. It's self-evident to hit back. Jesus' exhortation to reply to aggression with accommodation and submission is thus very striking: "And if someone wants to sue you and take your tunic, let him have your cloak as well. Give to the one who asks you, and do not turn away from the one who wants to borrow from you."

This message of suffering and non-violence has a certain popularity in our time. The peace movement has picked it up: don't we have here the means to break through the spiral of the arms' race? The Sermon on the Mount has been brought into position against the bomb. Verse 38 seems to verbalize the attitude which we have to get rid of once and for all: an eye for an eye and a tooth for a tooth. The modern balance of power, whose growth man is powerless to control, appears to be based on this principle of retribution: eye for eye, weapon for weapon, rocket for rocket. It appears just as clearly that Jesus rejects the thought of retribution replacing it with the message of non-violence which breaks through the spiral.

Now Jesus has certainly come in the service of a peace movement. The angels did not sing in vain "Peace on earth and good will towards men." The prophets already announced that the Lord God is working towards total disarmament. In chapter 2 Isaiah says that in the days of the Messiah the nations will beat their swords into plowshares. "Nation will not take up the sword against nation, nor will they train for war anymore." At the same time the Bible also demonstrates that this goal can only be reached through the coming of God's king and through submission to His Annointed Son. Men will not make any peace with one another if they have no peace with God; and nations will not be reconciled to one another before they are reconciled to their Creator. For that reason Jesus became man in order to suffer and to die for our sins. The disarmament of the nations demanded the death of the Savior. There is no other way to the kingdom of peace than via Jesus Christ. By faith we will receive world peace from Him when He returns in glory. Plucking texts out of the Sermon on the Mount without bowing before Jesus is unthinkable. Those who don't want to hear about sin and salvation may not write texts from the Sermon on the Mount on their banners. God has his own peace movement on this earth. Marching in it by faith we learn something underway about nonviolence from Jesus.

Right versus might

Jesus begins His instruction in verse 38 with a word that was spoken to the forefathers: "Eye for eye, tooth for tooth." They follow the proclamation of the Ten Commandments in Exodus 21:24. Although they sound harsh and unpleasant to our ears, we are nevertheless dealing with mild and fair regulations.

Violence is truly harsh, and violence has a long history in this world: as old as our fall into sin. Cain started with his bare fists and beat his brother to death. Lamech, one of his posterity, composed songs to violence and glorified it like an early "Hell's Angel:" "I have killed a man for wounding me, a young man for injuring me." No wonder then that his son, Tubal Cain, discovered the craft of smithing: the science of weaponry supports the man intent upon asserting himself.

Over and against the irrational violence of revenge and enmity God has taught man about right. Retribution must not be blind, or in rage, but rather fair and controlled. Justice means punishing every offense according to its seriousness. Killing a young man for one punch is not just: at the most the boy should have been punished with a similar slap. Self-controlled and impartial judges are needed to apply the rule of eye for eye. If fact, the whole concept of legal liability in modern times is nothing else than the application of the fair rule: eye for eye, compensation for damage suffered.

The people of Israel were held back from imperialism by the law of "eye for eye" while their kings were known as mild rulers.

Christian ethics have developed guidelines for a just war and one of them is keeping everything in proportion. Minor provocations do not justify major retaliation and total war (which is waged blindly) is in and of itself un-Christian.

Having penetrated into the human world through sin, violence is being pushed back by *right*, which God teaches man, and the law of fair retribution remains in force under Jesus' reign too. Indeed, the last judgment will employ it as the standard measurement: everyone will be judged according to his works and not arbitrarily punished. God will not destroy the world in rage but He will act as a righteous Judge. The Lord has shown how much this right is worth to Him by placing the priceless blood of His own, beloved Son over and against the unpayable guilt of man. The "eye for eye" rule brought Jesus instead of us to Golgotha, the place which God had forsaken. This manner of righteous retribution truly demonstrates that with God, right does not drive out mercy!

In modern discussions the balance of power is defended with the eye for eye rule. But the equation of the rule "eye for eye," "tooth for tooth" with the modern arms' race is certainly incorrect. Weapons developed to function as instruments of *total* destruction clearly violate the careful rule of eye for eye. The struggle of *right* against violence, even totalitarian violence, *degenerates* into a balance of terror when the limits of fairness and self-controlled response are exchanged for the intemperance of total destruction.

Non-violent faith

A superficial reading of verse 29 might give the impression that Jesus is ready *to trade in* the rule of right, (which must be brought into position over and against violence) for the rule of non-violence under opposition and oppression. After reminding his audience of "eye for eye" in verse 38, He begins to talk about non-violence in verses 39 to 42. This follows upon the word which the forefathers had already received, the message which He Himself intends to transmit. Still, Jesus does not intend to replace one rule with another. On the contrary, He places no new general rule over and against the general rule of eye for eye. At the beginning of verse 39 He declares that the rule of eye for eye must not be applied in the special case of the struggle against the evil one. The rule has not been abolished, but it appears to be inapplicable to the struggle against the evil one.

Here some interpreters read *all evil, wicked persons*. This can't be the case. Jesus would have then employed the plural form by speaking about all possible forms of persecution in His examples. The text would have read: "Do not resist evil persons but if someone strikes you on the right cheek, turn to him the other also." Something else is written there instead: "Do not resist *the evil one*. If someone strikes you on the right cheek turn to him the other also." At this point we need to think about Satan, the great opponent of God's kingdom of peace. One of the preceding verses (5:37) mentions his name and he resurfaces in the 6th entreaty: "But deliver us from the evil one" (6:13). In his attack against God Satan employs all kinds of people by inciting them against Christians whom he hopes to intimidate and lead away from the faith. Jesus had already spoken about people who "insult you, persecute you and falsely say all kinds of evil against you because of me" (5:11). Now that the evil one reappears on stage in 5:39, his instruments show up again in verses 39b to 42.

People may strike believers on the cheek (39b), obtain unjust settlements through lawsuits (40), condemn them to forced labor (verse 41) and demand and confiscate their possessions (42). Nevertheless, all of these pin-pricks delivered by hostile humans can be traced back to the enmity of the evil one against God's kingdom of peace and against all those who believe in it. Christians are not struggling against men, but against Satan. They should not attempt to assert their rights in this struggle now. In this front-line, they have to choose for suffering, non-violence. The requirement for people and nations to stand up for right and to punish violence fairly must remain. But Christ's church does not use this rule of justice in the struggle against the evil one. Here the requirement to suffer and accept persecution counts so that we might inherit the kingdom of heaven through great oppression, (5:10).

Jesus' strategy stands over and against the dormant zealotry of Israel: right up to the present day the Jewish people still have the urge to insure a place for themselves on earth by force. Jesus' marching orders also stand diametrically opposed to the idea of the holy war in Islam. While Israelis fight against Muslims, with a religiously charged fanaticism, the Christian church has had to follow the road of arena's and discrimination and forced labor. No swords are being forged in secret, only books of martyrs in public.

What is this non-violent faith good for anyway? It proves that the evil one has lost. No general gives his troops the order to lay down their weapons before the battle is decided. But since Jesus says this, it is apparently safe enough to proceed with suffering. He has overcome the evil one. Even the gates of hell cannot overcome His church. The calling of the church in the New Testament period is to demonstrate through non-violent life *how rock-solid* faith in Christ's triumph may be.

Because the church is weak, Jesus receives the honor: He is the one who rescues and preserves her in the battle which the evil one still wages against the church. Disarmament can begin with God's people: a sign of hope for a world which is still scourged by violence and still needs to employ the sword of righteousness.

God's demonstration for peace has started its march and continues, though many people don't feel inclined to join this kind of peace-movement and even throw mud at the believers.

Church and armament

Jesus' words about non-violence do not lead to universal pacifism. They focus on the struggle of believers against the evil one and their behavior under oppression and persecution. They teach the church not only to forgo any counterattack during oppression, but also give her the courage not to depend on the weapons of the world. In her struggle against the evil one the church has no need of a nuclear shield, neither directly nor indirectly. She is not called to seek out suffering but at the same time she may not try to keep it outside the door. Suffering and persecution do not represent failure for the church: she is allowed, if God so wills, to glorify Christ through her suffering. The persecuted church seeks no pity, but rather prayer and participation. The continued survival the non-violent Christian faith demonstrates to the nations of this world who really is sovereign on earth. At the same time it shows that He does not build His kingdom by means of violence, but through faith. That kingdom knows complete disarmament.

Believing in Jesus and waiting for His kingdom means breaking with violence, and being committed to pursuing right. God places us under the equitable rule of "eye for eye." As citizens

Christians will be devoted to the employment of justice as a weapon against violence, national and international. Intercessory prayer for judges is church prayer. Striving for righteousness, in the waging of war and armaments as well, belongs to a Christian's tasks. If Christians are not by definition pacifists, neither do they give their blessing to all weapons and sanctify each war. The reverse applies as well: Christians who suffer rather than fight for their faith can still help their neighbor when it concerns *just wars* against murderers and tyrants. At the same time they know that the struggle of right against might will only be brought to a conclusion in God's kingdom of peace. There true believers will go inside while murderers will stay outside forever (Rev 22:15).

9. Anti-Discrimination

> Be sons of your Father who is in heaven: He makes
> His sun rise on the evil and on the good.
>
> Matthew 5:43-48

Equal rights

Some words or phrases are very loaded in a particular time
or period. In our day and age that certainly applies to the terms
"discrimination" and "equal rights." Labeling something as "dis-
criminatory" amounts to a devastating condemnation, and nothing appears to be loftier than equal opportunity. Every difference
and every quality has been made subservient to it. The dif-
ferences between the races in talents, history and culture have
to be left completely outside of any consideration when dealing
with peoples and tribes. Whenever someone does not want to
see marriage made the equivalent of all kinds of "life-styles," he
will quickly be shouted down as an enemy of equal rights. Who
in the world wants to be an advocate of unequal rights?

The way in which the expressions "discrimination" and
"equal rights" are employed today is rooted in the doctrine of
human rights. All human beings have the same rights and for
that reason they ought to receive the same treatment too. At
the same time from the standpoint of human rights this also
means *identical* treatment.

Christianity, not based on any doctrine of human rights, is
now being judged more and more negatively. On the basis of
God's creation-order Christians differentiate the place and task
of man and woman. For many they have thereby become the
heretics of the 20th Century. Christians also make a distinction
between marriage as an institution established by God and a
homosexual relationship which violates God's creation-order and
commandment. Because of that many people consider Christians
to be the archvillains of the modern era: they discriminate!

In an attempt to save Christianity some take shelter in a
distinction between the Christians with their disputable Bible in-
terpretations and the Lord Jesus who in reality outlawed all
discrimination. Wasn't He just as much a teacher for prostitutes

51

and tax collectors as for the Pharisees? And didn't He abolish all forms of prejudice when He told about His heavenly Father who causes the sun to rise on the evil and the good? Is it possible to plug the Sermon on the Mount into the modern plea for complete toleration and the right of self-determination for every person?

Love and hate

Jesus begins His instruction in verse 43 with a reference to something spoken to the forefathers: "Love your neighbor and hate your enemy." That sounds harsh and at any rate it looks like discrimination: treat your neighbor and your enemy unequally! Many Bible interpreters have a hard time imagining that God could have ever said anything like that to the people of Israel. Correspondingly, the first section is ascribed to God: "Love your neighbor," while the second section is dismissed as an incorrect Jewish tradition: "Hate your enemy." Over and against this Jewish perversion of the golden rule Jesus is supposed to reveal God's true intentions again. It's hard to get around the fact, however, that Jesus was always quoting the Words of God in the previous sections when He talked about the things spoken to the forefathers. Should that be any different all of a sudden? Did not the Old Testament really teach love towards fellow Israelites and foreigners, but at the same time hate towards the enemies of God as well?

This double-edged commandment cannot be separated from the fact that God's people in the Old Testament constituted a nation with their own territory and their own king. Anyone with borders on this planet has to watch over them too. Invading enemies cannot be greeted as brothers. There will be war. Not out of a desire for conquest, but rather to protect God's land and God's people. Loving of one's people has as its flip-side hating all those who would wipe it from the face of the earth. Loving Israel means hating Haman!

Love versus hate

Jesus' appearance marks a turning point in history for God's people. He hands Israel a new order of the day: "But I tell you: love your enemies." A new sound because a new era is dawning. Not a time in which prejudices can be eliminated. The enemies of the church remain active. They shall "curse, hate, attack and persecute" the believers. That is terrible and it calls forth revenge, antipathy, counteraction and revolt. In the centuries before Jesus' coming in Israel this would have been sufficient grounds for God's people to call everyone to the flag and to give their persecutors their just rewards under the leadership of a Samson or a David. The new response Jesus is teaching Israel is quite striking: "Love your enemies, bless those who curse you, do good to those who hate you, pray for those who persecute you." Now the attitude of love, very active love, replaces the hatred of enemies. A wondrous counterattack.

Another era is clearly dawning. A time in which national territory will no longer have to be guarded and a time in which the church will no longer be gathered inside earthly boundaries. A time in which Jesus prepares His church for the kingdom of heaven of which the earthly Israel was a shadow. The struggle has already been decided: the enemy is powerless and on the run. Since Jesus' coming the gates of hell are no longer capable of overcoming His church. Now we have the room to love our enemies. We don't need to react negatively. We can show our faith in Jesus' victory through unconcerned love for our persecutors. Who wouldn't pray for losers who are going to perish? Who wouldn't be concerned for people who ought to be very worried. Christ's triumph frees His church to pray for its persecutors. Loving Christ, you no longer have to hate Herod!

Love without boundaries

By placing His people in the open, Jesus calls upon His subjects to mirror God's love in their lives without limits. "That you may be sons of your Father in heaven. He causes His sun to rise on the evil and the good, and sends rain on the righteous and the unrighteous" (verse 45). God gives His sun and His rain indiscriminately to all men. He causes His sun to rise unceasingly in Japan, over Siberia, Russia, Europe and all the way to the shores of the Americas. Regardless of the races which live there and regardless of the ideology they might hold: the sun rises. God is the One who allows the sun to rise! Not as a deadly heat. At precisely the right time He mixes drought and rain according to the circumstances and needs of every region. In this way the earth becomes fruitful and offers food and drink for man and animal. It's man's fault that not everyone enjoys this. God opens His hand without any restraint. He has done this through the centuries. Paul points this out to the pagans in Lystra. Even though they served idols in the preceding centuries, God did not leave himself without testimony: "He has shown kindness by giving you rain from heaven and drops in their seasons; He provides you with plenty of food and fills your hearts with joy" (Acts 14:17).

Christians are allowed to imitate this love. Not because all human beings are equal or because all people have the same rights. Jesus emphatically speaks about good and bad people, the righteous and the unrighteous. There is a difference. The one deserves help, the other does not. The basis for God's love lies in His patience and not in human rights. He does not employ His majesty to shut wicked people out of sunlight and food. He surrounds them with His care too because He still wants to lead them to repentance. The whole of world history represents a period of gracious sparing through limitless patience. One day that will all come to an end, at the last judgment. Now, however, is the time for repentance, and God's love invites everyone to do that. God's children must imitate that image. Even when they are persecuted. God Himself is cursed and hated by many: nevertheless, he allows His enemies to walk the streets in the sunlight. In this way Christians are allowed to do good to those who hate them. So that the world will catch a glimpse of the image of the Father through the response of their love. Since God allows His sun to shine over Red Square, we may pray for the atheistic rulers in the Kremlin.

Equal love for unequal men

Love among men is always limited. For that reason Jesus says: "If you love those who love you, what reward will you get? Are not even the tax collectors doing that? And if you greet only your brothers, what are you doing more than others? Do not even pagans do that? Be perfect, therefore, as your heavenly Father is perfect" (verses 46-47). The Israelites who kept the law cut themselves off from tax collectors and they in turn had their own circle of friends too. People draw borders around themselves: anyone falling outside their territory is dropped. Today it is no different. Whoever is unwilling to bow before a modern vision of equality, can forget about being treated equally. He will be actively discriminated against and unequally treated. By continuing to speak about good and evil, Christians will be unwelcome. Discriminating does not stop with those who employ the word "discrimination" as a defamation.

Jesus, however, teaches us how to treat all men without any discrimination. Not an equal opportunity which stands in awe of their human rights, but equal opportunity which passes God's love on to all, the good and the bad. "Be perfect, therefore, as your heavenly Father is perfect" (verse 48). The Bible forbids us to make any distinction between man and woman, or black and white, when it comes to manifesting love and doing good works.

True love adjust itself to the needs of others. Love never hurts anyone's feelings. Love does not send a neighbor away with freedoms he is incapable of handling. Love asks what is appropriate and what will help, and what is useful and edifying. God gives sun and rain using other criteria in the tropical lands than in North America. He changes the climate between the coast and the interior. At first glance inequality in treatment seems to abound. But if this inequality arises out of love and good care, and if it is the correct treatment, every land breathes again and every region can come to full bloom. Treating everyone exactly the same way is not very difficult: in point of fact we dismiss everyone with impersonal treatment. Treating everyone the correct way on account of love is very difficult: nevertheless, we then pull everyone towards us with non-discriminating love. This is the only kind of "equal rights" with a future, because it reflects the love of God.

10. Personal Faith

> But when you pray, go into your store-room and
> shut the door and pray to your Father who is in
> secret: and your Father who sees in secret will
> reward you.
>
> Matthew 6:1-18

A private affair?

More than ever before the 20th Century has pushed faith
to the private area of life. Personal opinions or mystical views
of life are permitted as long as they are kept out of public life.
Society and state are being secularized: faith has to be satisfied
with the inner room.

The rejection of God and His authority over our lives forms
the motif for this development. Belief is something personal and
free, as long as the believer does not give the impression of
adhering to an authentic worship of God: that would contain an
indirect appeal to all people because God, of course, stands above
everything. Modern man doesn't want anything to do with a God
like that and correspondingly Christians are expected to scale
their faith down to a private affair.

In the Sermon on the Mount Jesus speaks about a pull-back
to the inner room too. He, however, places this in a totally different context. His foremost concern is to include God rather
than keeping other people out. Everyone here has to make a
personal choice because our faith concerns the all-encompassing
reality of God. We will all come to stand before a living God who
will reward people for what they said and did. Our future depends
upon Him. Far from being a private affair, faith is a major
significance for the whole world. For that reason living with an
outward faith which suffices itself to fall in step with other people is inadequate: everyone needs the inner-room personally.
Not because faith is a private affair but because it places us in
front of no one less than the holy and almighty God Himself.
He sees the hidden corners of our personality: those areas have
to be filled up too.

Personal religion

The danger constantly facing the church is for faith to become a facade without a framework to support it. At that point the life of faith becomes roll-playing. In this regard Jesus uses the characterization "actors" three times in verses 2, 5 and 16: the translation "hypocrites" gives the impression of a false appearance. The term employed, however, points to play acting. That can be done in all sincerity. An actor can play his role perfectly. Only: the role is not the actor. The actor is often a completely different person than the one he portrays. Thus there are many who perform the part of "pious prayer" without also kneeling before God in their inner room. Jesus urgently warns us not to belong to those who act out their faith.

An actor performs in front of men, in front of an audience. In the same way a person can deliver a believing "performance" in front of his neighbors, church or world. Like the actors of that time trying to attract attention to their performances by blowing a trumpet, so also there were people who literally sounded a gong before they helped someone else, for example, with alms. The synagogues and street corners bore the inscriptions registering the names of those who had made a contribution to city or synagogue. Givers like that already have their reward: they harvest the desired applause during the performance of their act of charity.

Even prayer can become a one-act play in front of men: "But when you pray, do not be like the hypocrites, for they love to pray standing in the synagogues and on the street corners to be seen by men." They already have their applause: everyone admires their zeal for prayer.

Even humiliation before God through fasting can degenerate into a farce when a person shows everywhere his somber face. The person fasting makes himself unpresentable in order to show himself off to other men, (verse 16). No corner of religion is free of the danger of roll-playing aimed at men.

True religion, however, orients itself to God alone. The point of it all is that *He* sees us, and He sees us when other people do not. In our own room, in our free time, in the evening and at night. What are we like when the door closes behind us? Everybody has to face this tense question. God inspects men behind the scenes. Then it will become evident: was he an actor or a true believer?

In the Sermon on the Mount Jesus teaches how personal religion must be. At the mountain He instructs the people of Israel that decisions are not made at the temple but in the silence of everyone's personal life. Not because religion is a private affair, but because religion is in reality service to the living God who looks into the heart and sees its hidden corners. The passport of faith into the kingdom of heaven must bear our own name!

Helping in silence

Jesus gives three examples of how to experience personal religion. The first concerns mercy. He says: "But when you give to the needy, do not let your left hand know what your right hand is doing" (verse 3). Some translations restrict this verse to the giving of alms, but the word which Jesus uses is broader in scope. It encompasses giving to the poor and performing all kinds of services for people ill or in need. Aiding someone else should take place in silence. We don't need to count our good deeds on our fingers and we shouldn't congratulate ourselves with a pat on the back. Some people bubble over about all the help they have given. Jesus teaches us neither to openly brag in front of others nor to be inwardly satisfied with ourselves. We may not even secretly congratulate ourselves because we have helped someone else: don't let the left hand know what the right hand is doing. God alone will congratulate us for our mercy as reward for what we have done. But then our helping must be for Him, in secret and unnoticed, without a fuss about it either for ourselves or for others.

In practice, gifts and aid often quickly diminish without the presence of contributor lists and social control. At that moment the true value of our help comes out. When people cannot see what we do, the genuineness of our personal religion will become evident.

Significantly, Jesus' first example focuses on helping our neighbor. How will a man ever love God, whom he does not see, when he refuses, in silence and for God, to really help his brother, whom he does see. The first priority of our inner room for God is a hidden door to our neighbor. The commandment to love our neighbor is on par with the commandment to love God. The love for our neighbor forms the simplest measure of our religion.

Praying in the inner room

The second example which Jesus provides concerns prayer. Many prayers were uttered by the people of Israel, just like in the church today. But prayer does not yet thereby become personal service to God. Jesus says: "When you pray, go into your room, close the door and pray to your Father, who is unseen" (verse 6). Jesus uses a word which is often translated as "inner room." That translation might give the impression that every believer needs a large house containing a private bedroom for everyone, even children. Most of Jesus' listeners possessed only a small, one-room apartment. This word, however, does not go over their heads. Jesus is speaking about a store-room or cupboard. Every room has its special corner or basement for storing things. The family does not live there. You have to go out of your way to get there and having closed the door, you are standing in the dark: away from everything else. In that store-room, however, everything is lit up before God: praying in seclusion, hidden away. No one needs a private room for that. A small area, even dark, is large enough to reach to heaven. The first question for a believer is not whether he says grace at the table or prays along in church but whether he also prays all by himself. Prayer becomes pure religion in private. Prayer at the table and in the church loses its value before God, if we do not know or neglect to do it secluded away and in silence.

Personal prayer, more so than prayer in public, often ends up becoming an emphatic and repetitious request for many everyday, petty things. Praying then becomes a private plea for nice weather and good health, for everything we think that we need. For that reason Jesus also says the following about our personal prayer: "And when you pray, do not keep on babbling like pagans, for they think they will be heard because of their many words. Do not be like them, for your Father knows what you need before you ask Him" (verse 7-8). Nervous in their prayers, unbelievers don't know when to stop because they are uncertain as long as they do not possess. Jesus teaches us to pray in faith: Our Father knows quite well what we need. We don't need to spend many words and we can also rest assured in it. The form and content of praying in silence should make that apparent.

As a positive example Jesus then recites the prayer which

we know as "the Lord's Prayer." Twenty centuries of a praying church have given this prayer a tremendous depth of sound and association. You could easily write a book describing it as the crystal in which all the truths of the faith sparkle. While reading the Sermon on the Mount we need to keep in mind, however, that Jesus taught this prayer as an example of praying in private. Curiously enough, the Lord's Prayer has now become the most public prayer in the liturgy: it is often spoken in unison and out loud. It is perhaps the most little used prayer in the inner room too. That's odd. Jesus did not forbid us to bring inner-room prayer into the common liturgy. We forfeit something, though, when we no longer primarily view the Lord's Prayer as a personal prayer, in the darkness of the cellar. There it ought to regulate the heartbeat of our praying.

Over and against restless prayers for our private needs Jesus places a short and powerful prayer with which we can praise God. The Lord's Prayer is often divided into six sections, but in fact it begins with one, intensive three-part supplication for the coming of God's kingdom. When the promises made by John the Baptist are fulfilled, the era will dawn in which things on earth will be like those in heaven. In God's kingdom everyone will hallow His name and do His will. Having heard the good news that the kingdom of heaven is near because God's Son has appeared, we must repeatedly pray with heartfelt desire that God's glory really inundates the world now too. The second section of the prayer asks that we may be allowed to enter that kingdom as well. Our requests are minimal; daily rations for the road (daily bread), grace for sinners (forgive us), and safe-conduct for people who cannot make it on their own (deliver us from the evil one). In short we must learn that our personal prayer is aimed at God's coming and our entrance. We have to learn to pray in faith (thrice) and ask with self-understanding (in need). Shouldn't our prayer behind closed doors, kneeling before a bed or chair, be turned into the frequency of God's Gospel for us? When God hears the echo of His promises in our personal prayers, He will reward us accordingly. Whoever knocks at the right address: to him the door will be opened.

Hidden fasting

The third example which Jesus gives is closely bound up with the second one. Fasting and prayer belong together. In our time the term fasting is also used in pleading for the voluntary reduction of consumption for the sake of the environment and underdeveloped countries. Regardless of how good this might be, breaking with extravagance and luxury should not be termed "fasting." True fasting represents coming to repentance before God. For a few days or a few hours the prayer forgoes food and festivities in order to be completely devoted to humiliation and devotions. Fasting was common among the Jews, and Jesus does not abolish it. He says "But when you fast, put oil on your head and wash your face" (verse 17). Other people don't need to see it: only God does! Maybe the Jews thought: but who controls whether anyone fasts or not? Jesus wants to teach them that fasting has value only when it is done uprightly before God and not before men.

Fasting expresses an understanding of guilt before God. Knowing himself to be a sinner before his Holy Father, the faster covers himself in sackcloth and ashes. Whoever fasts renounces all his rights and throws himself as a supplicant before His Creator.

Even today fasting can turn into a show with dark suits, long faces and a lot of weeping in the church. As a reaction to this some have become proponents of a "happy" Christianity. Still, fasting before God is essential for "happy Christianity." A Christian knows how miserable and guilty he is before His God and how much he has to be forgiven. Jesus had already spoken about that in verses 14-15 following the Lord's Prayer. Prayer is a request to enter the kingdom of grace. Praying this is difficult if you are still hard-hearted against your own debtors, and fasting hooks up to this. Forgiving Christians are not gracious people because they easily let something go by, but because they know how heavily in debt they are to the heavenly and holy God. This makes them forgiving towards other debtors and drives them to fasting before God.

Since a fast must take place in secret, it cannot be identical with collective days of fasting. Nevertheless, it doesn't say much for their sense of guilt when Christians never see reason for personally abstaining from extra things or festivities without being required to.

By pointing to fasting in secret as demonstrating humility before God, Jesus shows that our physical posture in the innerroom takes on great significance. A supplicant *kneels*. God observes the preparations for our prayer and our posture. No man sees that: for that reason it is so important! Your Father, who sees what is done in secret, will reward.

Public reward

God rewards personal religion openly in His public kingdom. Then it will appear that true religion is not a private matter. Those who helped in secret will be shown mercy (5:7). Those who prayed silently while hungering and thirsting for righteousness, will be satisfied (5:6). Those who fasted and mourned here unnoticed will be comforted (5:4). Even the public reward in the coming kingdom of God is very personal.

11. Looking

> The eye is the lamp of the body. So, if your eye
> is sound, your whole body will be full of light.
>
> Matthew 6:19-24

Treasures in sight

In verses 19 to 24 Jesus talks about the radical choice for
the kingdom of heaven. At first glance there doesn't seem to
be much cohesion in the section which speaks about storing up
treasures (19-21), the significance of the eye (22-23), and the im-
possibility of serving two masters (24). Through changing images
and via divergent approaches, however, we encounter the theme
of the radical choice at the cross-roads. We stand between an
earthly and a heavenly treasure, between an eye full of darkness
and an eye full of light, between hating and loving. We have
to take the right decision decisively and continuously.

A choice is determined by our appraisal of the things in-
volved. Every person has his values. They may differ sharply according to age group, but various things always become priorities. They are "in," or "sought" or "preferred." At a certain stage
of life some things are ignored, while they are desired at another
stage. Some people cannot keep their eyes off of something while
others remain totally uninterested. Young and old attempt to
realize their goals and obtain what they judge to be important.
In Jesus' time many poor dreamed of possessing a fortune one
day. Wealthy and secure they would no longer be dependent
upon the caprices of the rich and powerful. They would do
anything to get their hands on a fortune. Wouldn't you be willing to live like a pauper if through that you were able to buy
a plot of land which you knew contained a hidden treasure? Who
wouldn't say farewell to family and friends in order to become
rich in another country? Even today immigrants are leaving
underdeveloped nations to gather what would be considered a
"treasure" of money in their home countries.

Jesus now compares searching for treasure with searching
for the kingdom of heaven. At first glance no one seems to profit
very much from it: more likely, faith, brings poverty and persecu-

tion. At closer examination, however, the opposite appears to be the case. Earthly treasure corrodes and perishes through moths and rust. Its vulnerability remains as well: others can always take it away from us through whatever form of theft or coercion. This does not apply to the luxury and glory of the kingdom of heaven: these things are elevated above the wear and tear of mortality and the threat of theft.

Jesus' instruction does not stress the value of the kingdom of heaven, but rather the question of how much value *we* attach to it. Jesus says: "For where your treasure is, there your heart will be also." The heart is the real issue. We will not persevere on our earthly journey to the kingdom of heaven unless we are totally pervaded by the future which awaits us. Everything must be made subservient to a desire to obtain the fullness of life and holiness in God's kingdom. Prospectors are afflicted with gold fever. Travelers to God's kingdom ought to be homesick for heaven. We know that the treasures in sight are for real!

Respect for the master

Anyone dealing in inanimate objects, draws up a scale of values. Silver is fine, but gold is more precious. Better a good salary than the minimum wage. We compare the comparable. When the issue concerns treasure on earth versus treasure in heaven, however, we are quite incapable of drawing up a list of priorities. As if the former is worth a bit more than the latter. The only choice possible is a radical one, and why? Because here we are choosing for one master and against another. While you can love both gold and silver, you cannot serve two masters at the same time: "Either you will hate the one and love the other, or you will be devoted to the one and despise the other." In this way we cannot "serve both God and Mammon."

Powers and masters stand behind the respective earthly and heavenly treasures. In the final analysis we will serve one or the other: God or Mammon. Mammon is a term applied to the idol of earthly possessions. Meaning possession, the word has been personalized to "Mammon." A power with a master in the background: the evil one or Satan. Aiming at our destruction, this ruler anonymously attempts to capture us with the gifts and possibilities of this world. In paradise the issue already concerned, so it seemed, not the services of Satan but a fruit worth eating and it is still the case that the possibilities and attractions of this world, at first glance totally neutral, are used to keep people from coming back to God and the desire for lasting treasures. Anyone with interest in earthly treasure falls into a trap. Walking before God, in His commandments and towards the coming kingdom of heaven becomes very difficult. You can only serve one master at a time.

Choosing for God also means that we stand differently over and against the possibilities and treasures of this earth. They become subservient to our preference for heavenly treasures. We can only serve one God in this life. The difference between Mammon and God is that the former hides himself while God makes Himself known. We know where we will end up with Him!

The gleam in our eye

Wedged between the statements about earthly versus heavenly treasure and the two masters we can find a few words concerning human eyes. Verses 22 and 23 are related to the radical choice as well. Jesus speaks about good eyes and bad eyes. Once again a parting of the ways, and the word "good" specifically points to the "simplicity" of our eyes. The Greek word is not generally found in conjunction with eyes. Jesus chooses it in order to allude to the subject of the unmixed and undivided choice for heavenly treasure. Eyes which don't look in two directions at once are appropriate for an unconditional choice: a single or good eye.

Jesus says: "The eye is the lamp of the body." A surprising statement. But we often hear such things from Jesus' mouth. Ordinarily we think of the eye as an organ which receives light, but not one that spreads it. Eyes have to catch light: they can't give it away, can they? Nevertheless, Jesus is speaking here about gleaming eyes. They fill the whole body with light, while false eyes darken it.

Using these drastic expressions about the eye as a lamp, Jesus focuses our attention upon the crucial significance of our vision. First, the eyes look, and then the feet move. Our eyes focus our attention and our body follows. The Bible is full of examples of bad eyes which darkened the whole body. Eve looked with a false eye at the only fruit which God had denied to man. She saw the attractive fruit. When she followed her wrong looking, her whole body became darkened: shame crept up between people and guilt overshadowed their birth and work. Michal, looked with a false eye at her husband, David, while he danced and jumped in front of the ark with the common people, and account of pride her life was made barren. Judas looked with a false eye when Mary expressed her love for the Savior with expensive perfume before His death, and the end came when he went and hung himself because he had betrayed innocent blood. Darkness is great when the eye is not good.

Our eyes have everything to do with looking forward to treasures in heaven and breaking with the service of Mammon on earth. Whenever our eyes are excited and stimulated by earthly riches, the body is carried away into the slavery of greed, or jealousy or lust or avarice. Those desiring to reach heaven had better be careful with their looking. The eye must be excited by the things of God and His future. When our eyes are uprightly trained on God, like the eyes of a slave girl trained to the hand of her mistress, our whole body will be enlightened to do all sorts of good works. Correct behavior begins with correct vision.

The visual man

According to many people man in the 20th Century is much more visually oriented than he was in earlier periods. The church should adjust itself accordingly. The era of preaching churches with listening services is past, and don't expect too much from traditional Bible reading. The future lies with seeing and with audio-visual communication. Whether or not man has always been a visually oriented creature is debatable. It could be the case that nothing has happened to our ears which somehow hear less, but that something has happened to our eyes and our seeing. Modern man looks a lot but sees little. His eyes have gone blind. Man refuses to have an eye for heaven, for God the Creator, for angels and devils, for a life after death and a last judgment. When the eye is bad because it refuses to look further than the visible horizon, life becomes darkened.

In this day and age it is good to learn that the eye is the lamp of our body. How we look and what we look at are of great importance. When our eyes are pure, we can look with joy at everything which is good and deserves praise: Seeing good examples teaches us to follow them. We will look with displeasure at those things which are worthless and speculate on the wrong attributes or feelings: we learn to have an aversion to evil. Correct vision keeps our life fresh while keeping a view of heavenly treasure open.

In this visually oriented era we have to learn that the eye is not a neutral receiving station, but a lamp for our body. This lamp must shine by aiming the eye at God, the only Master. An original motto we can hang on the book shelf or attach to the television is: "The lamp of the body is the eye. If your eyes are good, your whole body will be full of light."

12. Worrying About Tomorrow

> If God so clothes the grass of the field, which to-
> day is alive and tomorrow is thrown into the oven,
> will He not much more clothe you, O men of little
> faith?
>
> Matthew 6:25-34

Being worried or taking care?

Taking care for the future is human. At first sight Jesus almost seems to do away with our taking care for tomorrow in the Sermon on the Mount. There we read the following statements: "Who of you by being anxious can add a single hour to his life?" and "Do not be anxious about your life, what you will eat or drink, what you will wear." Does Jesus want to teach His listeners the careless ways of the vagabond?

The context of these statements produces something different. Caring for the future is not taken away but the horizon has been drastically shifted. Jesus says: "Your heavenly Father knows that you need them. But seek first His kingdom and His righteousness and all these things will be given to you as well." Food, drink and clothing remain the daily needs of human-beings and even God in heaven knows that and is concerned about it. We, however, have more important matters on our minds. Seeking God's kingdom takes priority over all our daily needs. The tomorrow for which we must provide is further away than today. Jesus teaches us to shift the attention of our concern for the future. He does not abolish our caring of the future, but He teaches us to do it with a forward-looking vision.

Some translations have clouded this somewhat. Through their headings and method of translation the translators then give the impression that Jesus is only speaking about anxiety. As if eliminating nervous and agitated anxiety from our worrying was the only thing that mattered, and that is important to a Christian too. A Christian does his work prayerfully rather than in desperation while handling his eating, drinking and clothing in faith. This point also shows up at the edge of Jesus' instruction concerning worrying in His fleeting reference to the heavenly Father who knows our earthly needs and takes care of them (32b and 33b). The primary matter in the Sermon on the Mount is something else. Jesus' teaching is not aimed in the first instance against false anxiety but against the false direction of our worrying.

The verb which various translations render "being worried" is in fact a neutral verb which means "being somehow busy with something, concerned with something." Jesus is not talking about the quality of our worry but about the object of our concern. That is very clear in verse 33: "Seek first His kingdom." That is the priority which we must learn.

Jesus has built an enormous tension into the section which leads up to verse 33. He repeats three different times that we should be unconcerned with eating, drinking, and clothing, and again the object to which our worrying should be directed remains unmentioned. Until the final word comes out in verse 33.

The first time we hear the following words: "Therefore I tell you, do not worry about your life, what you will eat or drink; or about your body, what you will wear. Is not life more important than food, and the body more important than clothes?" (verse 25). A somewhat shocking formulation of the question. We tend to think that life and body are more important than food and clothing, and therefore we devote so much attention to eating, drinking and clothing because our own life and body are worth it. Nevertheless, Jesus appears to want to direct our concern to matters other than sowing, reaping and storing away (verse 26). But what do life and body really need then?

Unanswered, the question is posed a second time from another standpoint. "Who of you by worrying can add a single hour to his life?" (verse 27). Once again a somewhat confusing question. Even if we are unable to force our bodies to grow, we still have to provide these things to prevent our bodies from collapsing and dying. Jesus, however, wants to consider things other than spinning and weaving (verse 28). What does He want us to do then?

Once again the question remains unanswered. In fact it returns to haunt us for the third time when Jesus picks it up again in verses 31 and 32: "So do not worry, saying 'what shall we eat?' or 'what shall we drink?,' or 'what shall we wear?' For the pagans run after all these things and your heavenly Father knows that you need them." Does Jesus intend to lead us either down the road of asceticism or that of carelessness?

The liberating word finally comes: "Seek His kingdom and His righteousness." Now it also becomes clear why He built up such a tension first. Left to themselves people become intensely wrapped up in the things of this life: good food and drink, a better house and a career. Each day multi-color advertisements hand out images of the things which we are supposed to worry about according to those who invent them for human consumers. Over and against the overwhelming attention for this life, Jesus has to make very clear to us, penetratingly and shockingly, that we need to aim at something better for life and body.

The beginning of verse 25 (Therefore I tell you) indicates that Jesus is going to give an explanation of striving for treasure in heaven (19-21). The new teaching of Jesus is: paying attention to the heavenly horizon is also the best thing for our earthly body and life.

The best thing for our bodies

Our time remains obsessed with physical health. Jogging keeps us in shape; the environmental movement also creates a demand for uncontaminated food and drink; the quality of food gets a lot of attention; the cosmetics' industry cares for our outward appearance with every means possible. Then that well-cared body can fit perfectly into the image created by the advertisements.

The Bible does not divert our attention from life and body. On the contrary, God created each one for us personally! But Jesus reminds us that we have fallen far behind. He points to the big lead which the animals have. Human beings have to sow, reap and store everything in warehouses the whole year round while birds fly around unconcerned, being nourished directly by God's hand. History shows that men can be able to live this unconcerned as well. Elija once walked through the wilderness for forty days and nights without food and was no worse off for it: God provided for him in the same way that He cares for birds and desert animals. Elija represents an exception. But not an extreme exception. Actually it should be normal that people are not dependent upon their labor and sweat. Today a man is in fact in service to himself: if he does not work, then there is no food. To fill his mouth he has to stoop over a shovel, in whatever form and enlisting the services of whatever other humans. We are used to that. It seems unavoidable.

But it used to be different. Only in Genesis 3, after the fall into sin, do we read about the necessity for man to work the earth in the sweat of his brow. The struggle against thorns and thistles has been placed like a yoke upon our shoulders. Before the fall man ate and drank from all the trees and streams which the Lord God allowed to grow or flow in the garden, and at the tree of life a man is as free as a bird. Having been present in Paradise Jesus' voice sounds very far away when He speaks about unimagined possibilities. Nevertheless, God will not allow man to remain in a state of servitude. The servant in the field will one day become the king over creation. Sounds from Paradise come blowing in like music for the future here and now. Will not God's children fly even higher than the birds? Will not He place them above the birds in His kingdom of heaven? Being dependent for food and drink our whole lives we can still try to make the best of it. But Jesus points to a better thing: life which is no longer subjected to hunger and thirst. Life in God's Paradise. Worrying about tomorrow for us means first and foremost finding the entrance to that kingdom in which man is free again.

Jesus compares our lives to those of the plants as well. They too are out in front of us. To obtain our clothes we still have to spin and weave. Our life hangs from a silken thread! The spinning wheel doesn't rest even if it has been moved to Taiwan. Man weaves multi-colored clothes for himself, and the most prominent people wear the nicest clothes. Ermine and precious stones are for the king. The luster of Solomon's royal robe must have been dazzling! Yet his robe cannot hold a candle to the colors of a simple flower in the field. Flowers *are* beautiful, people have to *make* themselves beautiful, and yet they still lose the contest. The flowers, however, never spin or weave. They just grow: no clothing industry springs up and no beautician arrives to help. People don't grow like that. We don't know any better.

Nevertheless, we once knew better. There was a time in which man did not need any clothing. His body was not yet really naked. After the fall into sin something changed: people began to be ashamed of themselves before others. The lustre is gone. Shame creeps upwards, and the Lord God teaches man to clothe himself. Although many people today may be proud of their clothes, the flowers of the field remind us that in reality it's all artificial, not genuinely our own. The nudist culture at the beach seems to signal the end of our culture.

A return to nature is impossible today. Still, a time is coming in which our nature will be culture again. Jesus promises that God, who already decorates the grass of the field so colorfully with flowers, will certainly adorn us. This therefore means that every believer in the kingdom of heaven will leave King Solomon far behind and finally will be able to compete with the beauty of the flowers in the field. Some primitive peoples paint their bodies with bright colors: feeling something is missing, they seem to want to compensate for it. The result is garish and forced. Whoever really wants to care for his body would be wise to turn his gaze to the Paradise of the kingdom of heaven. We know not yet what we shall see there!

In this context Jesus purposely employs the uncommon phrase "O you of little faith." Oftentimes Christians hardly dare to imagine anything in the future. When thinking about body and life, their hope and prayers appear to be limited to a reasonable preservation to this colorless body and a substantial lengthening of its years. The gospel, however, gives us higher expectations. Despite having little imagination concerning a redeemed life, we can certainly dream better things concerning the future. Paul, at the rate, knows that all things in creation, both plants and animals, strain their necks to look towards the time that people will once again be God's children on the earth. For that reason the marketplace of this time should not make us short-sighted: there are better bargains to be found for life and body than eating, drinking and clothing. They must be sought in the approaching kingdom of our God!

The first priority in our lives

When Jesus exhorts us to seek first the kingdom of heaven, He does not intend to say that this kingdom might be unfindable. We don't need to track it down. Jesus has come in order to reveal it. But we have to make an effort to be able to enter it. We must apply ourselves to faith and hope. When we know the right direction, then we still have to go that way and search out the high destination.

Verse 34 summarizes these words: "Therefore do not worry about tomorrow." Our lives must be aimed at God's kingdom rather than bound up in the worries of this life. Despising our earthly needs of food and clothing is unnecessary as long as we subject all these things to our conscientious search for God's great future in His kingdom of heaven.

"For tomorrow will worry about itself," Jesus says in following. That is to say: the future will arrive all by itself. God knows very well what we need here on earth and He is working on the victory of His kingdom of heaven. Jesus does not say that tomorrow has it own cares. The text reads: "Tomorrow will take care of itself." Tomorrow will worry about itself. This is no statement to make us apathetic (there is something everyday to keep you busy), but a word which gives us peace: the future will work out all right.

Now we can also understand the surprising conclusion to verse 34: "Each day has enough wickedness of its own." We purposely use the word wickedness here. Jesus is not speaking about the troubles of each day, of which there are of course many, but He is talking about the sins of every day. Surprisingly enough, a text which offers perspective for liberated human life suddenly ends in the deep valley of human wickedness. That is not really very strange though. We still have to *seek* the kingdom of God, and why do we have to look so hard even though it is close by? Because we have to overcome the powerful resistance of unbelief and our predisposition to all kinds of sins. The evilness of our own nature forms the great counter-current to searching for the kingdom of heaven. We should be very concerned about that. We have our work cut out for us. Without daily struggle against ourselves and our bent towards egotistic or dishonest words and deeds, we will not be able to persevere in the faith. That means: we will never reach the sought after kingdom of heaven.

The forward-looking gaze in our interest for body and life demands energetic action today. We would rather begin the struggle against sin tomorrow. But that is precisely the great worry for today. Whoever really wants to live and get himself into shape, can leave the worries about the future to God. He can concentrate on fighting sin in the day in which he lives. What appears to be a detour is in fact the only way to obtain a world where man will finally display the glory of God's creation. Man, although today the evilest thing in the world and causing pain to fellow man and environment, was nevertheless made as the zenith of creation. Jesus is returning there with His disciples too!

13. Me

First take the log out of your own eye!
Matthew 7:1-12

Me first

The time in which we live has been termed the me-generation.

Humanistic faith in man ends up as the individualism of the single person. Having pushed out God, humanity stands defenseless over against the tyranny of the individual: every ME demand his own space and freedom.

The reverse side of this is limitless toleration. Who am I to dare to intervene in the life of another person: isn't he or she just as free as I am? Toleration for everyone is the mirror image of the preference for myself. People give each other the freedom to do as they please in a pluralistic society in order to be able to make their own choices as well.

The Sermon on the Mount contains a phrase which appears to be grist for the mill for this modern toleration. It is short and to the point: "Do not judge." In the church Jesus' statement has been eagerly employed more than once in order to cast a shadow over efforts to keep both doctrine and life in the congregation pure. Are we allowed to condemn a pastor having a few strange ideas? In the same way people protect their life-style from instructions or admonitions of others. We aren't supposed to judge one another, are we?

In reality this represents a misuse of a quote from the Sermon on the Mount. Jesus isn't aiming at our neighbor to forbid him to be concerned about us. He is aiming at us. Neither does He do it to stand up for the freedom of our neighbor. Rather He is concerned for our future. The reason for the commandment lies in His fear that we might one day become the victims of our own judgment. Verse 1 says in its entirety: "Do not judge, or you too will be judged." Thereby Jesus is thinking about God's judgment. A judgment is certainly coming with a verdict concerning our words and deeds. Everyone must first examine himself because we will all be judged by God. Not in order to experience our own freedom and to guarantee it for others, but primarily to escape our own judgment before God.

The explanation contained in verses 2 to 4 shows again that the background to Jesus' speaking is God's judgment and not human freedom. The last judgment is coming: "For in the same way you judge others, you will be judged, and with the measure you use, it will be measured to you." There are measures and norms for judgment: life is neither value free nor to be filled in according to individual choice. Jesus does not intend to keep us from judging because there is nothing to be condemned, but rather because we have to begin with ourselves. "Why do you look at the speck of saw-dust in your brother's eye and pay no attention to the plank in your own eye?" My neighbor ought to remove the speck out of his eye. His life too must be subjected to God's law. But I am the first one in line: let me first give some attention to the misuse of my freedom before I start looking for the mistakes of another. We cannot ever justify ourselves before God by condemning someone else. The church will not be accepted in grace because it can criticize the world. A man cannot enter the kingdom of heaven by pointing to the sins of his neighbor.

Jesus teaches us the proper sequence: "You hypocrite, first take the plank out of your own eye, and then you will see clearly to remove the speck from your brother's eye." Me first. Not in the sense of: I get to do what I want first. But in the sense of: first my conversion. Only after that will I be humble enough to help someone else rather than condemn him. In the me-generation the other person disappears in a haze of apathy. By taking the road to conversion our neighbor resurfaces out of that mist becoming the object of our brotherly love. Whoever first learns to live by grace, can be graceful in dealing with the faults of another.

My measures

A word in Jesus' instruction now follows connecting up to this. Here too He warns against thoughtless conduct that turns itself against us: "Do not give dogs what is sacred, do not throw away your pearls to pigs. If you do, they may trample them under their feet and then turn and tear you to pieces." Taking this puzzling verse out of its context makes the passage very difficult to explain. The history of exegesis demonstrates that it could mean almost anything. We must, however, explain it in conjunction with the preceding verses. Using different images the text once again discusses the danger of holding something up in front of others (or animals) which may eventually lead to our own ruin.

The particular power of the images employed here must have immediately struck the first listeners. To them Jesus' words probably sounded extreme and absurd. After all, sacred things are for the priests. Everything which the Israelites dedicated to the Lord and did not burn on the altar, was designated for them. Only the priests are allowed to eat this sacred food at a sacred place. It's not for anybody else. Naturally there were borderline cases. Determining who could be reckoned to the family of a priest required a great deal of effort. However, it would never occur to anyone to heedlessly toss sacred food, the first fruits of the Lord, onto the garbage heaps outside for the stray dogs. It was inconceivable! Why? Because sacred food is for the priests alone: it is their privilege. The second example also leads to something absurd. Pigs were not raised in Israel and they were certainly not fed precious pearls. Perish the thought that a woman would throw her pearls (in those days *real* pearls) in the trough. Expensive jewelry is intended to be worn. Both images have the same flip-side: it is self-evident that the priest keeps the sacred things for himself and that a woman wears her own pearls.

Jesus says these things in connection with his insistence to first apply God's norms and revelation to our own lives. The images employed fit into this. Having been given God's revelation in His Holy Word we are intended to live from it. More than once the books of Proverbs compares God's wisdom for the whole of life to a necklace which we are supposed to wear ourselves. Whenever we adorn ourselves with faith and good works, the sacred can come into its own.

In Israel many held the law up to others without bowing to it themselves. Expressions like "This mob that knows nothing of the law" and "the Gentiles who do not have the law" were common. Israel firmly held the handle of the mirror and let others stare into it. Condemning others while justifying themselves. Like a Pharisee who is thankful for not being like a disreputable tax collector. Jesus turns against this misuse of God's Word. It will eventually lead to their own destruction. In the end God allowed Israel to be trampled under by the pagan Romans. By running a deficit in sanctification a Christian church more than once became the victim of Mohammedism to which it had once proudly held up the gospel.

The man who wants to cultivate himself finds the finest attire in God's commandments. They adorn a man. They bring out the best in him again as a creation of God. The true me-culture finds its norms with God.

My Father

In verses 7 to 11 Jesus speaks about prayer. He already spoke about this in chapter 6. Nevertheless, this is no tired repetition. Jesus now brings prayer into the discussion by joining it to His insistence to first live according to God's commandments *yourself* and to first remove the speck out of your own eye. That is difficult for us. In and of ourselves we are unprepared to do "good things" and to persevere in them. We are quicker to harness our lives to selfishness and egotism than to respect for God and love of our neighbor. We are faster to condemn what is wrong with our brother than to show what is good in our own lives . We can see here how important it is that Jesus makes us hesitant to judge. By doing it correctly, we will end up at ourselves.

There is only one way out here: through prayer to our heavenly Father. He will give good gifts (literally: the good things) to those who pray to Him for them (verse 11). No speck will disappear from our eyes without prayer to God. Commandments will not become pearls around our necks without help from our heavenly Father.

For that reason Jesus teaches us to go to God when we take a look at ourselves: "Ask and it will be given to you, seek and you will find, knock and the door will be opened to you." Earthly fathers, who are sinners, already know how to care for their children. They may not always get what they want, but no father will ever give stones or a snake instead of bread or fish. A child trusts that. How much more are we allowed to trust that our heavenly Father will never give us evil instead of good. He might give us something other than what we asked for, or at another time, but then it is always better and never worse for us.

Jesus has a purpose in moving the prayer in the direction of searching and knocking. It concerns arriving at and entering the kingdom of heaven. God's Word and His commandments are given for underway. We must learn to live from these commandments as a means of entering into God's kingdom by faith. The Bible shows us the door but prayer hands over the key. Whoever wants to preserve the treasure of the gospel, must call in the help of His Father. Just like the ex-Pharisee Paul has taught: "So I find this law at work: 'When I want to do good, evil is there with me. What a wretched man I am. Who will rescue me from this body of death? Thanks be to God through Jesus Christ our Lord!' "

My fellowman

It should be clear now why verse 12 can function as a concluding sentence. "In everything do to others what you would have them do to you. For this sums up the law and the prophets." Although He will one day judge us, God is now graciously giving us the time to look, knock and find. In this way we also have to help our fellow man in patience and love. Not condemning, but caring. Not as judges but as brothers. Just as our Judge wants to be our Father.

The whole Bible (the law and the prophets) is summed up here. The law and the prophets have not been given to us in order that we might deal harshly with one another, but to first find the road to God's grace ourselves and then to help our neighbor on his way. God's Bible wants to save before the judgment comes. In the same way we are called to promote our neighbor's interests like our own rather than to promote our own interests against our neighbor. God's me-culture creates a humane society in which love graciously exiles selfishness.

14. Deception

> Beware of false prophets, who come to you in
> sheep's clothing, but inwardly are ravenous wolves.
> Matthew 7:13-23

Dead end freeway

Traveling in the countryside and in foreign countries can acquaint us with disappointing roads. An attractive path traveling into the country appears to end at the corner of a field. A hopeful-looking mountain road can sometimes lead to nothing more than a difficult attempt to get the car turned around for the climb back down from a dead end. Actually we should have taken disappointments like this into account: that is the risk of the narrow road.

We would really be surprised if suddenly and unannounced a broad freeway ended without even a turn-off to a secondary road. Things like that don't happen. Given the intensity of the traffic and the generous width of the lanes, we don't even need to worry about such eventualities. That is the advantage of the broad road.

In order to reach a goal we generally try to avoid the narrow road while choosing the easy highways. But it is precisely the opposite if we intend to reach the heavenly goal. In the Sermon on the Mount Jesus teaches us that a broad road travels to destruction while a narrow road leads to life (verse 13-14). This road to the sun is toll-free but very secondary. Many people have great trouble even finding it. In fact, most of them take the broad road which is simple and readily accessible.

Jesus' instruction concerning the broad and the narrow road is not intended to scare us or deter us. He is not talking about an impassable road full of treacherous breaks and potholes. But the route it travels is difficult to locate. Jesus uses the gate as a parallel image: a wide gate leading to destruction and a narrow gate leading to life. A gate, of course, is an entrance. Everyone can walk through it. A narrow gate provides just as much an opening to the inside as a wide gate. Most importantly, however, you must walk with precision to the entrance of a narrow gate. Neither deviating to the right or to the left too much. We have to pay attention. That is the point of the symbol of the road. We cannot rely on the actions of others: like everybody else they are seeking admission via the broad road. But you must *find* the narrow road. Although criss-crossed by recognizable and well-traveled roads, the Palestinian hill-country also contained small paths to villages and fields, sometimes only marked by a couple of stones. Then it's necessary to be careful and pay attention to the marks in the sand or grass. While the wider road often travels around the village, that hardly traceable path leads to it. Whoever finds it, arrives at home.

Jesus' words represent a timely warning for the church which believes in Him. Wanting to be a Christian along with the others and wanting to come into heaven or onto the new earth later is insufficient. It is not enough to be believing or full of hope underway. We have to learn to read the road map and then to really put the map to use. Without looking for the right road ourselves, we can end up in perdition with a whole denomination full of people. On the way to God's kingdom the freeway is a dead end.

Faulty road signs

False lighthouses were once employed to cause ships to run aground in order to be subsequently plundered. Nothing is quite as treacherous on a journey as false road signs. This certainly applies to the road to God's future. Road signs and traffic police-men can be found there too. They are called prophets: in God's name they point the way. John the Baptist was the last prophet. A guide and pioneer without equal. He pointed the people to Jesus who came after him and in whom the forgiveness is to be found. Jesus Himself has also to warn the people of Israel about pseudo-prophets in the coming period. They are not genuine. They appear to be road signs, but they show the wrong road or at any rate fail to point out the good and the narrow way. These days many people follow the dead end, broad road in un-suspecting trust precisely because so many false prophets, pastors and theologians, are not presenting them with the narrow road God has chosen. The responsibility of pastors who take things too loosely is great.

Jesus' remarks about "false" prophets cause many to think in terms of mean and nasty people. But by taking a look around at the church through the ages and at the vast Christendom of this century, we can see that things don't look so bad after all. We certainly encounter a variety of opinions but they are often represented by friendly, charming people with the best of intentions. Coming from churches which repeatedly warned against false teaching and heresy, young people are often later very impressed that these so-called heretics appear to be quite agreeable when personally encountered at work or in the neighborhood. Although having different beliefs, these Christians seem friendly in their contacts and just as concerned about the future of church and faith. But why should that surprise us? Jesus does not warn us about mean people: we keep an eye out for types like that all by ourselves. He is properly speaking about people who outwardly look like sheep. No one is maintaining that they purposely camouflage themselves. Jesus simply ascertains: their exterior is Christian. Perhaps uprightly meant. However, whether intentional or not, they are like ferocious wolves. Dangerous for the flock.

How does that become manifest? In the fruits of their work. Jesus says: "By their fruit you will recognize them. Do people pick grapes from thorn bushes, or figs from thistles?" (verse 16). Some expositors apply this to the behavior of false prophets. They might speak well, but they live falsely. This cannot be the case. Not only does Jesus say that they have a sheep's voice, but that they look like sheep too. Thus their actions and behavior give no indication of bad fruit in their own lives. But the issue does not center on the fruits in their own lives, but in the lives of others. They intend, of course, to be prophets and a prophet attempts to influence others with his word. Good prophets bring about sanctification in the people. When large groups of Jews went out to the Jordan to let themselves by baptized after confessing their sins, one could see therein the fruits of the prophet John the Baptist. The prophet was recognized by these fruits: a real man of God. Naturally the Old Testament knew many false prophets who preached peace while allowing the people to remain in their sins. They brought a message of "cheap grace." The fruits of their work were also apparent: church-goers brimming with injustice and arrogance. The fruits revealed the false prophets. Pious people, but in the meantime the flock took a beating.

Jesus teaches us to test the road signs. They may look good

and mean everything well and they may speak frankly and freely about the way to the kingdom of heaven; but when they do not tell the travelers about the narrow road which everyone must obediently follow, then they have become nothing than false lighthouses, and thereby the ship of the church runs aground. Even when everyone marches in unison towards a large Christian ecumenism, uncritical breadth can be just as deadly for God's children as the wolfsclaws of atheistic enemies. For whenever Christ's narrow road and the obedience to His commandments are not proclaimed as absolutely entrance requirements, we will end up in the valley of death. For that reason Jesus' disciples must be prepared to deal with unsound pastors.

The guide

The narrow road which we must find in order to go in is the road of Christian sanctification. "Not everyone who says to me, 'Lord, Lord' will enter the kingdom of heaven" (verse 21). Jesus now speaks without reservations concerning His authority as the Guide. The whole of the Sermon on the Mount is immersed in Jesus' authority. The tone betrays it: He rules in the church of God ("But I tell you"). Up to the end of the Sermon on the Mount He avoids speaking specifically about this authority. Now, however, He does. Jesus considers it proper that we call Him "Lord, Lord." Since the Jews at the mountain did not stand in a position of human subservience to Jesus (He was not their earthly employer), the title "Lord, Lord" must then indicate that Jesus wants to be addressed as divine law-giver. No wonder the Jews were quite shocked by what He said, "Hear O Israel, the Lord is God, the Lord Alone." Is this Jesus the Lord in our midst? John the Baptist had already said that the Lord Himself would come: now Jesus lets it be known that He is also Israel's God: He and the Father are one.

In verse 22 Jesus openly speaks about prophesying and performing miracles "in my name." Prophets then always spoke in the name of the Lord, prophets now shall speak in the name of Jesus Christ.

Moses in Egypt did wonders and signs in the name of the Lord; the apostles shall now do great miracles and cast out demons in Jesus' name. God's authority and power are working in and through His Son Jesus.

For that reason the decision about entrance into the kingdom of heaven lies in Jesus' hand too. His Father's kingdom belongs to Him as well. Jesus is the one who shall soon say to some publically that they are not welcome with God because He, Jesus, never knew them (verse 23).

Why does Jesus speak so frankly about His divine majesty at the end of the Sermon on the Mount? Because He is now placing the full weight of His authority in the scales over and against deceptive pastors. When hired-hands allow the flock to get lost in the wilderness, the Good Shepherd stands up and lets His voice be heard. Over and against the false lighthouses stands Jesus who is the Light of the world. Whenever we hear His voice and love Him, we will follow Him and not men, even when they are many in number or are lead by Christian-looking pastors.

Only one thing can help against the danger of deception: that we know Jesus and that *He* knows us. He knows all those who exert themselves to find the narrow but continuous road of the commandments which His Father has given us. Others may fail to appreciate this and consider it to be old-fashioned or legalistic, but God's Guide recognizes His worshipers and seekers. He gives them more than a Christian appearance. He gives them entrance to the Father. Acquaintances come inside. The road which leads to life is narrow but whoever does the will of Christ's Father will find it and be let inside. God's good guide is also the gracious doorkeeper.

15. The Safe House

> Everyone who hears these words of mine and does them will be like a wise man who built his house upon the rock.
>
> Matthew 7:24-27

Living in life

Men dwell in this life, they build themselves a house. Animals only nest from year to year. Or they have a hole to hide in or spend the night. But men build houses in order to live in them. Their whole life is like a house that they set up for themselves. We can also say that someone's house of life has been torn down when his work disappears, he loses his family, his health collapses. Some people are said to have "made it" in life, while others have made a "shambles" of theirs. However it may be, men want to live their lives.

At the end of the Sermon on the Mount Jesus also compares man to a house builder. It is a picture of what we make of our life and of its framework. But Jesus does not differentiate between successful and failed lives, between expensive homes and broken-down apartments. He only differentiates between safe and threatened lives, and this dividing-line runs right down the middle of everything else. Jesus does not ask what we have made of life and how successful our house of life looks, but He does ask how its foundation has been layed. Do we live in safety?

The greatest risk

Jesus' words concerning building on rock or on sand are directed by the thought of one threat which is moving towards all houses and all human life: the deluge of the flood. An image for God's judgment which will come over all life without regard for anybody.

According to some Bible expositors Matthew is speaking about the Palestinian fall storms which turn dry river-beds into strong currents, while Luke has adjusted the picture to surroundings outside Palestine by speaking about a flood (Luke 6:48-49). In fact, Matthew is talking about an unexpected large flood too.

If the passage were only concerned with the winter course of streams and rivers, then the man who built on sand would have been very foolish for erecting his house on the dry summer-bed of a stream. Jesus says, however, that he lived on the sand and not on the river bottom. That was not enough to hold off a calamity when wind and flood attacked the house at the same time.

The unexpected aspect of this disaster belongs to the overall picture. Whenever strong dikes give way in a night of storm, people are quick to say that an unfavorable combination of tide and wind power like that was not expected and should be viewed as abnormal. Jesus warns about what men actually do not expect and what they don't reckon with when building a house. The calamity of God's great judgment will one day come over the earth, and a house regardless of how strongly built, will not stand up to it unless that risk has been calculated in advance. Nevertheless, God's righteous judgment is coming over every human life, and over everything built, whether people viewed it as successful or not.

What was the mistake of the man who built on sand? Everyone builds on sand, don't they? The foolish builder did not loose his mind, like the man in the verse: "He wasn't very nice, and built his house on the ice." If you are that dumb, you can also expect to lose your house when the winter weather disappears. But the man in Jesus' parable is a good builder. He builds on good sand: a firm foundation. Good enough for this life and for a house like that. He is only missing one thing. He has failed to reckon with the outside chance of a hurricane wind in combination with a flood. Theoretically a disaster like that could occur, but who takes a very improbable risk into consideration now? In this way many people wisely build their house of life while neglecting to take into consideration whether God might exist and whether His judgment might one day strike. They have not calculated this risk as a risk for their own lives, and precisely that becomes their downfall. What appears to be the most unlikely possibility today, is the most certain event of the future. The man who builds on sand is negligent, and the consequences are serious: "The rain came down, the streams rose, and the winds blew (a deluge which no one ever took seriously into account) and beat against the house; and it fell with a great crash." The last words leave us staring into a gaping pit. The deluge still came. Thus Noah was right, and all life which had not taken that into account perished in the flood. The greatest danger for man is the danger in which he does not believe.

Well thought out life

The opposite of the man who builds on sand is the man who builds on rock. According to some Biblical interpreters Matthew is speaking about two different kinds of building sites (sand, rock) while Luke is concerned with a house that may or may not be built with a proper foundation (Luke 6:48-49). In reality Matthew also discusses a man who dug a foundation to the deeper lying rocks underneath (verse 25: it had its foundation on the rock). Of the two builders one builds more safety into his house, and that is the point, by digging further in order to let the foundation settle on the deeper-lying stone-bottom underneath the layer of sand. Isn't it a bit overdone to anchor a middle-eastern house like this: as if it would have to hold up in the ocean. But, of course, it will have to. The wise man prepares himself for the test by fire. For that reason he invests a great deal in the depth of the foundation.

This is a picture of the man who hears Jesus' words and does them. He lives a thought-out life. He knows that no human life can stand before God and for that reason he anchors his whole life in honor for Jesus the Savior and in loving His commandments.

The Bible does not dictate how to build our house of life brick by brick. God created us as responsible men. We have to build ourselves. Copying another man's walls makes no sense unless we lay a deep foundation in our own soil right down to the rock. Foundations are the unseen portion of a house, even though they determine its form and sturdiness. Jesus makes an appeal to our responsibility with His instruction about the wise builder. Living our lives demands thinking through to God, our Creator, our Judge and also our Savior.

Safe housing

Why does the house, well-thought-out when built, stand up against the deluge? Because the rock holds and carries it. In the Old Testament the Lord is often called the Rock of Israel. He carries His people. In this way Jesus now promises that His teaching will be the rock for the church in the new covenant.

The person who takes Jesus' commandments to heart when arranging his life can say: "He is my Rock, I will not be afraid, even though the waters swirl around me." Our own obedience will not save us, but rather it is the Rock upon which we build through faith which holds us fast. Anchored in Christ our life can withstand the judgment and inherit the kingdom of heaven.

In his epistle to the Romans (8:38-39) the Apostle Paul testifies to the security in his life thanks to the foundation upon which he builds: "For I am convinced that neither death nor life, neither angels nor demons, neither the present nor the future, nor any powers, neither height nor depth, nor anything else in all creation will be able to separate us from the love of God that is in Christ Jesus our Lord."

The Sermon on the Mount points the way to God and gives us the commandments of God's Son. Whoever takes this Sermon on the Mount to heart will live forever in a safe house.

Study Guide for the Sermon on the Mount

In the same way that shorter and longer hikes can be planned from a central position on a map, so too the following study guide provides various "reading paths" in the Bible with the Sermon on the Mount as the starting point. The reader should begin by choosing a passage from the Sermon (together with the discussion of it in this book) and then study the sections of the Bible listed here in days that follow. At the conclusion of this the reader can reconsider the passage which functioned as the starting point. It goes without saying that this roster composed of selected passages around specific themes only intends to offer a variation on book by book Bible study whereby the Scriptures are read in their unity.

1. *Faith is obedience* (Matthew 5:1-2).
1.1 In paradise already: Genesis 2:4-17.
1.2 After the Exodus from Egypt too: Deuteronomy 8.
1.3 It is wisdom: Proverbs 2.
1.4 Prophets point to it: Isaiah 1:10-20.
1.5 Jesus' high priestly prayer is aimed at it: John 17.
1.6 Grace requires it: Romans 6.
1.7 The last judgment proves it: Matthew 25:14-46.

2. *Happiness* (Matthew 5:3-12).
2.1 Blessed are the poor in spirit: Isaiah 61.
2.2 Blessed are they that mourn: Psalm 90.
2.3 Blessed are the meek: Psalm 37.
2.4 Blessed are they which do hunger and thirst after righteousness: Romans 7:7-25.
2.5 Blessed are the merciful: James 2:1-13.
2.6 Blessed are the pure in heart: Mark 7:1-23.
2.7 Blessed are the peacemakers: Romans 14:13—15:13.
2.8 Blessed are they which are persecuted: I Peter 3:13-18; 4:12-19.

3. *Israel* (Matthew 5:13-16)
3.1 Abraham for the nations: Genesis 11:1-9; 12:1-8; 18:16-19.
3.2 Israel for the world: Numbers 14:1-23.
3.3 The nations blessed through Israel: I Kings 10:1-13; Psalm 87.

3.4 Tasteless salt: Acts 7:30-53.

3.5 Continuous light: Romans 9:1—10:13.

3.6 Permanent task: Galatians 4:21—5:15.

4. *The Bible as Building-Program* (Matthew 5:17-20).

4.1 A lamp for underway: II Peter 1:12-21.

4.2 A word concerning realities: Hebrews 1:1—2:4.

4.3 A word in order to educate: II Timothy 3:1-17.

4.4 A Bible being fulfilled: Hebrews 12:18-29.

4.5 A Bible as example: I Corinthians 10:1-13.

4.6 The book of Christ: John 5:19-40.

4.7 Christ is the Word of God: Revelation 19:9-16.

5 *Dealing with others* (Matthew 5:21-26).

5.1 No fellowship without forgiveness: I John 1:1—2:2.

5.2 Service to God begins with our neighbor: I John 2:3-17.

5.3 Hating our brother is homicide: I John 3:11-24.

5.4 Love comes from God: I John 4:7-21.

5.5 Love takes precedence everywhere: Romans 13:8—14:12.

5.6 Love remains: I Corinthians 13.

6. *Marriage and faithfulness* (Matthew 5:27-32).

6.1 Marriage reflects Christ's love: Ephesians 5:15-33.

6.2 Marriage demonstrates Christian love: I Peter 2:19—3:17.

6.3 The bond of marriage and family: Matthew 19:1-15.

6.4 Contra infidelity: Proverbs 7.

6.5 Contra dishonesty: Ephesians 4:17—5:14.

6.6 Contra negligence: I Corinthians 7:1-24.

6.7 Self-discipline: Hebrews 12:1-17.

6.8 Love is tender: Song of Solomon 7:6—8:4.

7. *Honesty* (Matthew 5:33-37).

7.1 Speaking the truth requires a bridled tongue: James 3.

7.2 Honesty purifies relationships: James 5:12-20.

7.3 Love instead of lies: Colossians 3:5-17.

7.4 No religion without honesty: Zechariah 7 and 8:9-17.

7.5 Lies call forth violence: Proverbs 30:1-14.

7.6 Truth nourished by wisdom: Proverbs 4.

7.7 Honesty lasts forever: Psalm 15 and 24.

8. *Disarmament* (Matthew 5:38-42).

8.1 God's law protects man from his neighbor: Exodus 21:12-36; 23:1-9.

8.2 The promised peace of God: Micah 4 and 5.

8.3 Suffering as the way of Jesus' church: I Peter 1.

8.4 Christ's strength revealed in weakness: II Corinthians 4.

8.5 The suffering church supports the struggle for right: Romans 12:12—13:7.

8.6 Satan's war against Christ's church: Revelation 12:13—13:10.

8.7 The battle for the world has already been won: John 16:16-33.

9. *Anti-Discrimination* (Matthew 5:43-48).

9.1 A foreigner is not yet an enemy: Deuteronomy 24:10-22; 28:1-10.

9.2 No loving your neighbor without hating your enemy in the Old Testament: Psalm 18.

9.3 Christ can also pray for those who kill Him: Luke 23:33—24:9.

9.4 God's patient love in this world: Acts 14:8-18; 17:22-34.

9.5 General Christian love: Titus 2:11—3:11.

9.6 Love reconciles social conflicts: Philemon.

10. *Personal religion* (Matthew 6:1-18).

10.1 God's majesty makes us humble: Job 38 and 39.

10.2 Knowledge of self leads to repentance: Psalm 51.

10.3 God begins with our personal life: Ezekiel 18.

10.4 Personal prayer is not individualistic: Daniel 9.

10.5 Personal faith begins with our neighbor: James 1:19-27.

10.6 Personal faith comes our in prayer: James 1:1-18.

10.7 Personal faith and fasting: James 4:1-10.

10.8 Personal religion: Revelation 3:14-22.

11. *Looking* (Matthew 6:19-24).

11.1 Looking with understanding: Deuteronomy 4:1-20.

11.2 Appearances deceive: Psalm 73.

11.3 Earthly treasures bind: Matthew 19:16-30.

11.4 No one can serve two masters at the same time: Matthew 22:1-14.

11.5 The bad eye: Genesis 39:6-20 and Acts 8:9-24.

11.6 Faith sees what still cannot be seen: Hebrews 11:1-16.

12. *Worrying about tomorrow* (Matthew 6:25-34).
12.1 Caring about the blessing: Genesis 22:1-18.
12.2 The panorama for believers: Isaiah 55.
12.3 The desire of creation: Romans 8:12-30.
12.4 The better body: I Corinthians 15:35-58.
12.5 Seek first the kingdom of God and its righteousness: I Corinthians 6:9-20.
12.6 The future as profit: I Timothy 6:3-19.

13. *Me* (Matthew 7:1-12).
13.1 Shall I avenge myself?: Matthew 18:21-35.
13.2 The law is for me: Romans 2.
13.3 The purpose of the Bible: I Timothy 1:3-20.
13.4 Helping graciously: Galatians 5:13—6:10.
13.5 Judge not lest ye be judged: II Samuel 12:1-14.
13.6 God's wisdom: a jewel for our own use: Proverbs 3.

14. *Deception* (Matthew 7:13-23).
14.1 The true test of our faith: Deuteronomy 13.
14.2 The audacity of a deceitful spirit: I Kings 22:1-28.
14.3 Evil fruits from lying prophecy: Jeremiah 23:1-32.
14.4 The Good Shepherd gathers the scattered people: Ezekiel 34.
14.5 Leaders unmasked: Matthew 23.
14.6 Propagandists for the broad road: II Peter 2.
14.7 The narrow way is safe: I John 2:15—3:8.
14.8 No room in the church for wrong information: Revelation 2:18-29.

15. *The safe house* (Matthew 7:24-27).
15.1 Taking precautions in faith: Genesis 6:9—7:24.
15.2 The future is being forged today: Matthew 24:36—25:13.
15.3 A well thought-out plan for life: Jeremiah 35.
15.4 Perseverance: Hebrews 10:19-39.
15.5 The fire nears: II Peter 3.
15.6 Jesus confirms the conclusion to the Sermon on the Mount at the end of the Bible: Revelation 22:6-21.

Suggested further reading:

A classic example of exegetical sermons about the Sermon on the Mount is D.M. Lloyd-Jones *Studies in the Ser-*

mon on the Mount (1959 - 1960) Grand Rapids, 1981.

A more recent work is D.A. Carson's *The Sermon on the Mount*, Grand Rapids, 1984 (Second Edition).